Southern
TRADITIONS

100 years of
recipes from the
Martha White® Kitchens

Pillsbury Publications

The Pillsbury Company

Publisher: Sally Peters
Associate Publisher: Diane B. Anderson
Martha White Writer and Editor: Mindy Merrell
Martha White Editor, Spokesperson and Southern Food Historian: Linda Carman
Senior Food Editor: Andi Bidwell, C.C.P.
Recipe Editors: Nancy A. Lilleberg, Sandy Nieman, Nikole Officer Rutzen, Grace Wells
Contributing Writer: Dawn Carlson
Photography: David Damer Photography, Rutherford Studios
Photography Coordinator: Karen Goodsell
Recipe Typists: Renee Axtell, Bev Gustafson, Mary Prokott

Martha White Brand Development:
Marketing: Steve Moss, Mariann Hohe, Margarita Ortega
Promotions Managers: Tom Brown, Dean Evenson, Jennifer Kompelien
Sales: Alex Píña, Mark Hammond
Public Relations: Marlene Johnson, Sheryl Nagel-Anderson, Jackie Peterson

Photograph on page 49 courtesy of the Hatch Show Prints, a division of the Country Music Foundation.
Photographs on pages 11 and 216 courtesy of The Grand Ole Opry.

For more recipes and food information about Martha White Foods, Inc., visit our web site at
http://www.marthawhite.com.

Cover Food: Beans and Greens under Cornbread, page 98

Creative Publishing international
Minnetonka, MN 55343

President: David Murphy
Vice President, Custom Services: Sue Riley
Director, Custom Marketing and Publishing: Hugh Kennedy
Account Manager: Marie Kruegel
Art Director: Jann Williams
Copy Editor: Sandra Granseth
Photographer: Chuck Nields, Rex Irmen
Food Stylists: Abby Wyckoff, Sue Brosious, Sue Finley, Amy Peterson
Prop Stylist: Coralie Sathre
Studio Service Manager: Marcia Chambers
Photo Services Coordinator: Carol Osterhus
Project Manager: John Fletcher
Traffic Manager: Pete Skophammer
Production Manager: Janell Schmidt

Printed by World Color, U.S.A.
ISBN: 0-86573-171-3

TABLE OF CONTENTS

Easy Sour Cream Drop Shortcake, page 205

Celebrating 100 Years with Martha White

Heritage

Martha White Foods is celebrating a century of good Southern home cooking. Since 1899, the company's famous self-rising flour, corn meal and baking mixes have been trusted staples in kitchens across the South. With a salute to the rich legacy of the Southern table, Martha White Foods proudly begins its next 100 years. Goodness gracious, it's good!

Yes, the little girl whose name became synonymous with Southern baking was a real person. Richard (Uncle Dick) Lindsay, Sr., founded the Royal Flour Mill in Nashville, Tennessee, in 1899 and named his finest flour for his three-year-old daughter, Martha White. In 1941, when Cohen Williams acquired the Royal Flour Mill, he promptly changed the company name to reflect the name of their most popular brand. The little girl logo has changed over the years, but her picture remains a familiar face in homes across the South and still stands for the finest baking tradition.

ASK THE MARTHA WHITE KITCHENS

For almost 50 years Southern families have relied on the Martha White Kitchens for new recipes and helpful home cooking advice. It all started back in 1952 when owner Cohen Williams wanted to encourage home cooks to discover the versatility of self-rising flour and corn meal mix made with "Hot Rize." That's when home economist, Alice Jarman, started the Martha White Kitchens. Alice began the tradition of developing good basic recipes using everyday on-hand ingredients—the kind that have become family favorites. The kitchens quickly became the centerpiece of the company and a trusted authority on Southern home cooking. In fact, many of Alice's recipes are enduring classics today. Since Alice's retirement, Linda Carman has proudly carried on the traditions of the original Martha White Kitchens.

HOT RIZE®

In 1953, the trademarked phrase Hot Rize was coined to promote the convenience of the Martha White self-rising products. The leavening agent activated by oven heat offered consistent results to Southern bakers. Everywhere it was used—on product bags, on the Grand Ole Opry, on television commercials—Hot Rize soon became synonymous with the Martha White self-rising flour and corn meal.

Biscuits

Good Southern cooks make good biscuits, and these biscuits come in many forms. From big, thick "cat heads" to the crisp, thin variety, biscuits all begin with three ingredients—self-rising flour, shortening and milk or buttermilk. Personal preferences vary according to family tradition and region. Some cooks swear by buttermilk, others can't do without real lard; but good Southern biscuits always start with Martha White Self-Rising Flour with Hot Rize®. Take two, and butter them while they're hot.

Glazed Sugarplum Biscuits, page 17

Martha White Hot Rize® Biscuits

Martha White Hot Rize® Biscuits

This Martha White classic may be made with regular milk or buttermilk. Buttermilk biscuits have a slightly softer texture and a tangy flavor.

Prep Time: 30 minutes

> **2** cups Martha White® Self-Rising Flour
> ¼ cup shortening
> ¾ cup milk

1. Heat oven to 450°F. Lightly grease cookie sheet. Place flour in large bowl. With pastry blender or fork, cut in shortening until mixture resembles coarse crumbs. Add milk; stir with fork until soft dough forms and mixture begins to pull away from sides of bowl.

2. On lightly floured surface, knead dough just until smooth. Roll out dough to ½-inch thickness. Cut with floured 2-inch round cutter. Place biscuits with sides touching on greased cookie sheet.

3. Bake at 450°F. for 10 to 12 minutes or until golden brown. Serve warm.

Yield: 14 biscuits

OLD-FASHIONED BUTTERMILK BISCUITS: Substitute ¾ cup plus 2 tablespoons buttermilk for milk; add ¼ teaspoon baking soda to flour, if desired.

The Martha White Biscuit Technique

Biscuit-making is an art well worth mastering. And there's really nothing difficult about it. The Martha White Kitchens have helped generations of Southern cooks master the technique with these easy steps.

STIR THE FLOUR before measuring to loosen it, which will help make the biscuits light and fluffy. Measure the flour by lightly spooning it into a measuring cup.

CUT IN SHORTENING with a pastry blender (or two knives in a crisscross cutting motion) until the mixture looks like coarse crumbs. Cutting in distributes bits of shortening throughout the flour before the liquid is added. As the biscuits bake, the shortening melts in pockets which produce the tender, flaky layers. For extra-flaky biscuits, leave the shortening in larger-pea-size chunks. Lard or butter may be substituted for the shortening.

MIX by making a well in the dry ingredients and adding the liquid all at once. Stir with a fork only until a soft ball of dough forms and the mixture leaves the sides of the bowl. The dough should be soft. If dough is dry, add an additional 1 to 2 tablespoons milk. Using buttermilk instead of milk will give the biscuits a tangier flavor and moister texture.

KNEAD by turning the dough out onto a floured surface or pastry cloth. Roll dough around to lightly coat it with flour. Knead just enough to thoroughly combine the ingredients, 10 to 12 times.

ROLL dough with a rolling pin to an even ½-inch thickness. Biscuits double in height during baking.

CUT with a floured cutter. Push any leftover dough scraps together and gently reroll.

BAKE in a preheated 450°F. oven on a shiny, lightly greased baking sheet for a golden crust. Dark cookie sheets will cause the biscuits to over-brown on the bottom. For crusty sides, place 1 inch apart. For soft sides, place biscuits close together. Brush hot biscuits with melted butter or margarine, if desired.

Cheese Biscuits

Prep Time: 30 minutes

  2 cups Martha White® Self-Rising Flour
  ¼ cup shortening
  **4 oz. (1 cup) finely shredded sharp
       Cheddar cheese**
  ½ teaspoon dry mustard
  **⅛ teaspoon ground red pepper
       (cayenne)**
  ¾ cup milk

1. Heat oven to 450°F. Lightly grease cookie sheet. Place flour in large bowl. With pastry blender or fork, cut in shortening until mixture resembles coarse crumbs.

2. Stir in cheese, dry mustard and ground red pepper. Add milk; stir with fork until soft dough forms and mixture begins to pull away from sides of bowl.

3. On lightly floured surface, knead dough just until smooth. Roll out dough to ½-inch thickness. Cut with floured 2-inch round cutter. Place on greased cookie sheet.

4. Bake at 450°F. for 10 to 12 minutes or until golden brown. Serve warm.

Yield: 14 biscuits

Famous Buttermilk Biscuits

Just a touch of sugar and a bit more shortening make these tender morsels a little richer than most biscuits.

Prep Time: 30 minutes

  2 cups Martha White® Self-Rising Flour
  1 teaspoon sugar
  ⅓ cup shortening
  ¾ cup plus 2 tablespoons buttermilk*
      Melted butter or margarine

1. Heat oven to 450°F. In large bowl, combine flour and sugar; mix well. With pastry blender or fork, cut in shortening until mixture

resembles coarse crumbs. Add buttermilk; stir with fork until soft dough forms and mixture begins to pull away from sides of bowl.

2. On lightly floured surface, knead dough just until smooth. Roll out dough to ½-inch thickness. Cut with floured 2½-inch round cutter. Place on ungreased cookie sheet.

3. Bake at 450°F. for 12 to 14 minutes or until golden brown. Brush tops of hot biscuits with melted butter. Serve warm.

Yield: 12 biscuits

TIP: * To substitute for buttermilk, use 2½ teaspoons vinegar or lemon juice plus milk to make ¾ cup plus 2 tablespoons.

Fast Food-Style Biscuits

Prep Time: 30 minutes

  4 cups Martha White® Self-Rising Flour
  ¾ cup shortening
  1⅔ cups buttermilk*
      Melted butter or margarine

1. Heat oven to 450°F. Grease large cookie sheets. Place flour in large bowl. With pastry blender or fork, cut in shortening until mixture resembles coarse crumbs. Add buttermilk; stir with fork until soft dough forms and mixture begins to pull away from sides of bowl.

2. On lightly floured surface, knead dough just until smooth. Roll out dough to ½-inch thickness. Cut with floured 2¾-inch round cutter. Place on greased cookie sheets.

3. Bake at 450°F. for 10 to 12 minutes or until light golden brown. Brush tops of hot biscuits generously with melted butter. Serve warm.

Yield: 20 biscuits

TIP: * To substitute for buttermilk, use 5 teaspoons vinegar or lemon juice plus milk to make 1⅔ cups.

Biscuits and Bluegrass

From the beginning, Martha White Foods knew its customers well—they liked country music nearly as much as they liked biscuits and cornbread. The company's first advertising effort in the 1940s was the 5:45 a.m. country and bluegrass music radio show on WSM in Nashville. Known as "Martha White Biscuit and Cornbread Time," it was on when early bird Southerners were eating biscuits to start their day. It was also the radio spot where many country stars—Chet Atkins, Marty Robbins, Flatt and Scruggs, and the Carter Family—got their starts.

MARTHA WHITE AND THE GRAND OLE OPRY

In 1948, with an advertising budget of only $25 per week, Martha White Foods first sponsored a segment on Nashville's famous Grand Ole Opry, radio's longest-running show. In fact, the company has sponsored more than 2,500 broadcasts of the popular Saturday night radio program and today remains the show's oldest continuous sponsor. Over the years, the Martha White portion of the show has been hosted by country music's legends such as Flatt and Scruggs, Whisperin' Bill Anderson, Little Jimmy Dickens, Porter Wagoner and Roy Acuff. And Opry announcers, such as Grant Turner, became stars in their own right. Today, a portion of the historic "Martha White" backdrop, once used on stage at the Opry, is part of the permanent collection of the Country Music Hall of Fame in Nashville.

TOP: Folks line up for the Grand Ole Opry at the historic Ryman Auditorium in downtown Nashville, Tennessee.
BOTTOM: Lester Flatt and Earl Scruggs and the Foggy Mountain Boys sing during the Martha White segment of the Grand Ole Opry.

Corn Meal Supper Biscuits

A little self-rising corn meal mix added to a basic recipe gives these biscuits a heartier texture that stands up to robust soups and stews.

Prep Time: 35 minutes

1½	**cups Martha White® Self-Rising Flour**
½	**cup Martha White® Self-Rising Corn Meal Mix**
1	**teaspoon sugar**
⅓	**cup shortening**
¾	**cup plus 2 tablespoons buttermilk***

1. Heat oven to 450°F. Lightly grease cookie sheet. In medium bowl, combine flour, corn meal mix and sugar; mix well. With pastry blender or fork, cut in shortening until mixture resembles coarse crumbs. Add buttermilk; stir with fork until soft dough forms and begins to pull away from sides of bowl.

2. On lightly floured surface, knead dough just until smooth. Roll out dough to ½-inch thickness. Cut with floured 2-inch round cutter. Place on greased cookie sheet.

3. Bake at 450°F. for 10 to 12 minutes or until golden brown. Serve warm.

Yield: 14 biscuits

TIP: * To substitute for buttermilk, use 2½ teaspoons vinegar or lemon juice plus milk to make ¾ cup plus 2 tablespoons.

Sausage Show-Offs

Prep Time: 15 minutes (Ready in 50 minutes)

2	**cups Martha White® Self-Rising Flour**
¼	**cup shortening**
¾	**cup milk**
1	**lb. bulk pork sausage**

1. Heat oven to 350°F. Lightly grease cookie sheet. Place flour in large bowl. With pastry blender or fork, cut in shortening until mixture resembles coarse crumbs. Add milk; stir with fork until soft dough forms and mixture begins to pull away from sides of bowl.

2. On lightly floured surface, knead dough just until smooth. Roll out dough to a 14x10-inch rectangle, about ⅛ inch thick.

3. On sheet of waxed paper, spread sausage to 13x9-inch rectangle. Invert onto dough rectangle; peel off waxed paper. Beginning with long side, roll up jelly-roll fashion. Cut into ½-inch-thick slices. Place slices cut side down and 1 inch apart on greased cookie sheet.

4. Bake at 350°F. for 30 to 35 minutes or until biscuits are golden brown and sausage is no longer pink. Serve warm.

Yield: 30 biscuits

Three Reasons to Make Biscuits

1. If you can make biscuits, you can bake almost anything. This simple dough provides the foundation for many Southern favorites including dumplings, scones, cobblers, sweet rolls, coffee cakes, casseroles, shortcake and more.

2. Biscuits are a convenience food in homemade disguise. They're made with just three handy ingredients and bake in less than 15 minutes. You can whip them up anytime.

3. Everyone likes hot homemade biscuits. Make your friends and family happy.

Corn Meal Supper Biscuits

Cinnamon Buttermilk Biscuits

Prep Time: 35 minutes

BISCUITS
- 2 cups Martha White® Self-Rising Flour
- ¼ cup sugar
- 1 teaspoon cinnamon
- ¼ teaspoon baking soda
- ⅓ cup shortening
- ½ cup dried currants or raisins
- ¾ to 1 cup buttermilk*

FROSTING
- ¾ cup powdered sugar
- 2 to 3 teaspoons milk

1. Heat oven to 450°F. In large bowl, combine flour, sugar, cinnamon and baking soda; mix well. With pastry blender or fork, cut in shortening until mixture resembles coarse crumbs.

2. Stir in currants. Stirring with fork, add enough buttermilk until soft dough forms and mixture begins to pull away from sides of bowl.

3. On lightly floured surface, knead dough until no longer sticky. Roll out dough to ½-inch thickness. Cut with floured 2½-inch round cutter. Place biscuits with sides touching on ungreased cookie sheet.

4. Bake at 450°F. for 10 to 15 minutes or until light golden brown. Cool 5 minutes on wire rack.

5. Meanwhile, in small bowl, combine powdered sugar and enough milk for desired frosting consistency. Frost warm biscuits. Serve warm.

Yield: 12 biscuits

TIP: * To substitute for buttermilk, use 2¼ to 3 teaspoons vinegar or lemon juice plus milk to make ¾ to 1 cup.

Thimble Biscuits

Prep Time: 30 minutes

- 2 cups Martha White® Self-Rising Flour
- ¼ cup shortening
- ¾ cup milk
- ¼ cup jam or jelly

1. Heat oven to 450°F. Lightly grease cookie sheet. Place flour in large bowl. With pastry blender or fork, cut in shortening until mixture resembles coarse crumbs. Add milk; stir with fork until soft dough forms and mixture begins to pull away from sides of bowl.

2. On lightly floured surface, knead dough just until smooth. Roll out dough to ¼-inch thickness. Cut with floured 2-inch round cutter. Place half of rounds on greased cookie sheet.

3. With thimble or other small cutter, cut a small hole in center of remaining rounds. Stack rounds with holes on top of rounds on cookie sheet. Fill each hole with about ¼ teaspoon jam.

4. Bake at 450°F. for 10 to 12 minutes or until golden brown. Serve warm or cool.

Yield: 14 biscuits

Bacon Biscuits

Prep Time: 30 minutes

- 8 slices bacon
- 2 cups Martha White® Self-Rising Flour
- ¼ cup shortening
- ¾ cup milk

1. Heat oven to 450°F. Lightly grease cookie sheet. In large skillet, cook bacon over medium heat until crisp. Drain on paper towels.

2. Place flour in large bowl. With pastry blender or fork, cut in shortening until mixture resembles coarse crumbs. Stir in cooked bacon. Add milk; stir with fork until soft dough forms and mixture begins to pull away from sides of bowl.

3. On lightly floured surface, knead dough just until smooth. Roll out dough to ½-inch thickness. Cut with floured 2-inch round cutter. Place on greased cookie sheet.

4. Bake at 450°F. for 10 to 12 minutes or until golden brown. Serve warm.

Yield: 14 biscuits

Easy Cinnamon Rolls

Prep Time: 20 minutes (Ready in 40 minutes)

ROLLS
2	cups **Martha White® Self-Rising Flour**
¼	cup shortening
¾	cup milk
½	cup sugar
2	teaspoons cinnamon
¼	cup butter or margarine, melted

ICING
1	cup powdered sugar
1	tablespoon milk
½	teaspoon vanilla

1. Heat oven to 425°F. Grease 9-inch round cake pan.* Place flour in large bowl. With pastry blender or fork, cut in shortening until mixture resembles coarse crumbs. Add milk; stir with fork until soft dough forms and mixture begins to pull away from sides of bowl.

2. On lightly floured surface, knead dough just until smooth. Roll out dough to 14x10-inch rectangle, about ⅛ inch thick.

3. In small bowl, combine sugar and cinnamon; mix well. Brush dough with melted butter; sprinkle evenly with sugar-cinnamon mixture. Beginning with long side, roll up dough jelly-roll fashion. Cut into ¾-inch-thick slices; place in greased pan.

4. Bake at 425°F. for 18 to 20 minutes or until golden brown. Cool about 2 minutes.

5. Meanwhile, in small bowl, combine all icing ingredients; stir until smooth. Drizzle icing over warm rolls.

Yield: 18 rolls

TIP:* Rolls can be baked in greased muffin cups for 12 to 15 minutes or until golden brown.

Cinnamon Twists

Prep Time: 30 minutes
2	cups **Martha White® Self-Rising Flour**
¼	cup shortening
¾	cup milk
1	cup sugar
2	teaspoons cinnamon
½	cup butter or margarine, melted

1. Heat oven to 450°F. Lightly grease cookie sheet. Place flour in large bowl. With pastry blender or fork, cut in shortening until mixture resembles coarse crumbs. Add milk; stir with fork until soft dough forms and begins to pull away from sides of bowl.

2. On lightly floured surface, knead dough just until smooth. Roll out dough to ¼-inch thickness. Cut with floured doughnut cutter. Remove holes; reroll.

3. In small bowl, combine sugar and cinnamon; mix well. Dip biscuit rings in melted butter; dip in sugar-cinnamon mixture. Twist rings once; place about 1 inch apart on greased cookie sheet.

4. Bake at 450°F. for 10 to 12 minutes or until golden brown. Serve warm or cool.

Yield: 14 cinnamon twists

Easy Poppy Seed Drop Biscuits

Prep Time: 25 minutes

>   2 cups Martha White® Self-Rising Flour
>   2 tablespoons poppy seed
>   1 teaspoon sugar
>   1 cup sour cream
>   3 tablespoons butter or margarine,
>   melted

1. Heat oven to 450°F. Grease large cookie sheet. In medium bowl, combine flour, poppy seed and sugar; mix well.

2. Add sour cream and butter; stir with fork until dough forms. Drop dough by heaping tablespoonfuls onto greased cookie sheet.

3. Bake at 450°F. for 10 to 12 minutes or until golden brown.

Yield: 16 biscuits

Scones—the Biscuits' British Cousin

Scones, the biscuits' British cousins, come in as many styles as do biscuits. In general, though, scones are sweet and often flavored with dried fruits or nuts, and they have a more dense texture than biscuits.

In Great Britain, scones traditionally accompany afternoon tea. In the South, scones are a great alternative to sweet rolls or coffeecake.

Cranberry Scones, recipe page 20

Sugar-Crusted Sweet Potato Biscuits

Prep Time: 15 minutes (Ready in 35 minutes)

>   2   cups Martha White® Self-Rising Flour
>   4   tablespoons brown sugar
>   3   tablespoons shortening
>   ⅔   cup milk
>   ½   cup mashed canned or cooked
>   sweet potato
>   ⅓   cup sour cream

1. Heat oven to 400°F. Spray cookie sheet with nonstick cooking spray. In medium bowl, combine flour and 2 tablespoons of the brown sugar; mix well. With pastry blender or fork, cut in shortening until mixture resembles coarse crumbs.

2. In small bowl, combine milk, sweet potato and sour cream; blend well. Add to flour mixture all at once, stirring just until moistened. (If dough is too dry, add additional milk 1 teaspoon at a time, until dry ingredients are moistened.) Drop dough by ¼ cupfuls onto sprayed cookie sheet. Sprinkle with remaining 2 tablespoons brown sugar.

3. Bake at 400°F. for 15 to 20 minutes or until biscuits are golden brown. Immediately remove from cookie sheet. Serve warm.

Yield: 12 biscuits

Glazed Sugarplum Biscuits

A few easy additions such as dried fruit bits and a simple, sweet icing transform a basic biscuit into this delicacy.

Prep Time: 40 minutes

BISCUITS

2	**cups Martha White® Self-Rising Flour**
1/4	**cup sugar**
1/4	**teaspoon baking soda**
1/3	**cup shortening**
1	**cup dried fruit bits**
1/2	**cup slivered almonds, toasted***
3/4	**cup buttermilk****

GLAZE

1	**cup powdered sugar**
2	**tablespoons milk**
1/4	**teaspoon almond extract**

1. Heat oven to 450°F. In large bowl, combine flour, sugar and baking soda; mix well. With pastry blender or fork, cut in shortening until mixture resembles coarse crumbs. Stir in fruit bits and almonds.

2. Add buttermilk; stir just until dry ingredients are moistened. Add additional buttermilk 1 tablespoon at a time, if dough is dry.

3. On lightly floured surface, knead dough until no longer sticky. Roll out dough to 1/2-inch thickness. Cut with floured 2 1/2-inch round cutter. Place biscuits on ungreased cookie sheets.

4. Bake at 450°F. for 10 to 15 minutes or until light golden brown. Cool 5 minutes on wire rack.

5. Meanwhile, in small bowl, combine all glaze ingredients; stir until smooth. Spoon glaze over warm biscuits. Serve warm.

Yield: 23 biscuits

TIPS: * To toast almonds, spread on cookie sheet. Bake at 350°F. for 5 to 7 minutes or until golden brown, stirring occasionally. Or spread almonds in thin layer in microwave-safe pie pan. Microwave on HIGH for 4 to 7 minutes or until golden brown, stirring frequently.

** To substitute for buttermilk, use 2 1/4 teaspoons vinegar or lemon juice plus milk to make 3/4 cup.

Easy Scones

Prep Time: 30 minutes

1	**(7-oz.) pkg. Martha White® Muffin Mix, any fruit flavor**
1/4	**cup buttermilk***
1	**tablespoon butter or margarine, melted**
	Butter or margarine, softened
	Sugar

1. Heat oven to 400°F. Grease cookie sheet. In large bowl, combine muffin mix, buttermilk and melted butter; stir just until soft dough forms.

2. On lightly floured surface, knead dough just until smooth. Shape into smooth ball; flatten into 5-inch round. Brush with butter. Sprinkle with sugar. With floured knife or pizza cutter, cut into 8 wedges. Place wedges on greased cookie sheet.

3. Bake at 400°F. for 8 to 10 minutes or until golden brown.

Yield: 8 scones

TIP: * To substitute for buttermilk, use 3/4 teaspoon vinegar or lemon juice plus milk to make 1/4 cup.

Scottish Oat Raisin Scones

Prep Time: 20 minutes (Ready in 45 minutes)

- **2 cups Martha White® Self-Rising Flour**
- **½ cup rolled oats**
- **⅓ cup firmly packed brown sugar**
- **½ cup shortening**
- **⅓ cup raisins**
- **1 egg**
- **¼ cup buttermilk***
- **1 teaspoon vanilla**

1. Heat oven to 375°F. Lightly grease large cookie sheet. In large bowl, combine flour, oats and brown sugar; mix well. With pastry blender or fork, cut in shortening until mixture resembles coarse crumbs. Stir in raisins.

2. In small bowl, beat egg. Add buttermilk and vanilla; blend well. Add to flour mixture; stir just until blended. (Mixture may be crumbly.)

3. On lightly floured surface, press dough together to form ball; knead gently 8 to 10 times. Place dough on greased cookie sheet; pat into 8-inch round. With floured knife or pizza cutter, cut into 8 wedges. Separate wedges slightly, about ½ inch apart.

4. Bake at 375°F. for 18 to 22 minutes or until golden brown. Serve warm or cool.

Yield: 8 scones

TIP: * To substitute for buttermilk, use ¾ teaspoon vinegar or lemon juice plus milk to make ¼ cup.

Golden Raisin Scones

Prep Time: 20 minutes (Ready in 40 minutes)

- **2 cups Martha White® Self-Rising Flour**
- **2 tablespoons sugar**
- **½ cup butter or margarine**
- **1 cup golden raisins**
- **¾ cup buttermilk***
- **1 egg, separated**
- **Sugar for topping**

1. Heat oven to 375°F. Grease large cookie sheet. In large bowl, combine flour and 2 tablespoons sugar; mix well. With pastry blender or fork, cut in butter until mixture resembles coarse crumbs. Stir in raisins.

2. In small bowl, combine buttermilk and egg yolk; blend well. Stirring with fork, add enough buttermilk mixture until soft dough forms and mixture begins to pull away from sides of bowl.

3. On lightly floured surface, knead dough just until smooth. Divide dough in half; shape each half into smooth ball. Place balls on greased cookie sheet; flatten each into 6-inch round. With floured knife or pizza cutter, cut each into 6 wedges; do not separate.

4. In small bowl, beat egg white until foamy. Brush tops of scones with egg white; sprinkle with sugar.

5. Bake at 375°F. for 18 to 20 minutes or until golden brown. Serve warm.

Yield: 12 scones

TIP: * To substitute for buttermilk, use 2¼ teaspoons vinegar or lemon juice plus milk to make ¾ cup.

Scones with Devon Cream

Prep Time: 25 minutes (Ready in 45 minutes)

SCONES

 2 cups Martha White® Self-Rising Flour
 2 tablespoons sugar
 1 teaspoon grated orange peel
 ¼ teaspoon baking soda
 ½ cup buttermilk*
 ¼ cup butter or margarine, melted
 1 egg, lightly beaten

DEVON CREAM

 1 (8-oz.) pkg. cream cheese, softened
 ⅓ cup sour cream
 1 tablespoon sugar

 Strawberry preserves, if desired

1. Heat oven to 400°F. Lightly grease cookie sheet. In large bowl, combine flour, 2 tablespoons sugar, orange peel and baking soda; mix well. Add buttermilk, butter and egg; stir with fork just until dough pulls away from sides of bowl.

2. On lightly floured surface, knead dough just until smooth. Divide dough in half; press each half into ½-inch-thick round. With floured knife or pizza cutter, cut each into 8 wedges. Place wedges about 1 inch apart on greased cookie sheet.

3. Bake at 400°F. for 15 to 18 minutes or until golden brown.

4. Meanwhile, in small bowl, combine all Devon cream ingredients; beat until smooth. Serve warm scones with Devon cream and strawberry preserves.

Yield: 16 scones; 1¼ cups Devon cream

TIP: * To substitute for buttermilk, use 1½ teaspoons vinegar or lemon juice plus milk to make ½ cup.

Orange Almond Scones

Prep Time: 20 minutes (Ready in 40 minutes)

 2 cups Martha White® Self-Rising Flour
 ⅓ cup sugar
 2 teaspoons grated orange peel
 ⅓ cup butter or margarine
 ½ cup milk
 ¼ teaspoon almond extract
 1 tablespoon milk
 ¼ cup sliced almonds

1. Heat oven to 400°F. Lightly grease large cookie sheet. In large bowl, combine flour, sugar and orange peel; mix well. With pastry blender or fork, cut in butter until mixture resembles coarse crumbs.

2. In small bowl, combine ½ cup milk and almond extract; blend well. Add to flour mixture; stir just until blended. (Mixture may be crumbly.)

3. On lightly floured surface, press dough together to form ball; knead gently 8 to 10 times. Roll out dough to ½-inch thickness. Cut with floured 2½-inch round cutter. Place on greased cookie sheet. Brush tops with 1 tablespoon milk; sprinkle with almonds.

4. Bake at 400°F. for 16 to 20 minutes or until golden brown. Serve warm or cool.

Yield: 12 scones

Sour Cream Scones

These scones make wonderful shortcake. Serve them with sweetened fresh strawberries or peaches.

Prep Time: 15 minutes (Ready in 35 minutes)

- 2½ **cups Martha White® Self-Rising Flour**
- ¼ **cup sugar**
- ½ **cup butter or margarine**
- 1 **egg, beaten**
- 1 **(8-oz.) container sour cream**

1. Heat oven to 400°F. Lightly grease large cookie sheet. In large bowl, combine flour and sugar; mix well. With pastry blender or fork, cut in butter until mixture resembles coarse crumbs.

2. In small bowl, beat egg; blend in sour cream. Add to flour mixture; stir just until blended. (Mixture may be crumbly.)

3. On lightly floured surface, press dough together to form ball; knead gently 8 to 10 times. Roll out dough to ½-inch thickness. Cut with floured 2½-inch round cutter. Place on greased cookie sheet.

4. Bake at 400°F. for 16 to 20 minutes or until golden brown. Serve warm or cool.

Yield: 15 scones

Cranberry Scones

Prep Time: 25 minutes (Ready in 50 minutes)

SCONES

- 3 **cups Martha White® Self-Rising Flour**
- ½ **cup sugar**
- 1 **teaspoon grated orange peel**
- ½ **cup butter or margarine**
- 1 **cup fresh or frozen cranberries, halved**
- 1 **egg**
- ⅓ **to ½ cup buttermilk***

ORANGE BUTTER

- ½ **cup butter or margarine, softened**
- 2 **tablespoons powdered sugar**
- 1 **teaspoon grated orange peel**

1. Heat oven to 400°F. Grease large cookie sheet. In large bowl, combine flour, sugar and 1 teaspoon orange peel; mix well. With pastry blender or fork, cut in ½ cup butter until mixture resembles coarse crumbs. Stir in cranberries.

2. Place egg in 1-cup measuring cup; beat well. Add buttermilk to make ⅔ cup. Add to flour mixture; stir gently with fork until dry particles begin to cling together. (Do not add more liquid. Mixture may be crumbly.)

3. On lightly floured surface, gently press dough together to form ball. Divide dough in half. Place both halves on greased cookie sheet; flatten each into 6-inch round. With floured knife or pizza cutter, cut each into 8 wedges. Separate wedges slightly, about ½ inch apart.

4. Bake at 400°F. for 20 to 25 minutes or until golden brown. Cool on cookie sheet 5 minutes.

5. Meanwhile, in small bowl, combine all orange butter ingredients; blend well. Serve warm scones with orange butter.

Yield: 16 scones; ½ cup orange butter

TIP: * To substitute for buttermilk, use 1 to 1½ teaspoons vinegar or lemon juice plus milk to make ⅓ to ½ cup.

Cranberry Scones

Cornbread

Cornbread was North America's first bread, sustaining Native Americans for thousands of years before the arrival of Europeans. While other regions of the U.S. can lay claim to breads made from the indigenous grain, it's the South that perfected cornbread.

Who knows why? Perhaps a hot skillet of cornbread—crusty brown on the outside, moist and tender on the inside—is just another good example of folks in the South making the best of what they had.

Martha White Southern Sausage Cornbread, page 27

Cornbread Basics

What is really good Southern cornbread? It's soft and moist on the inside with a deep golden brown crust on the outside. The three necessities for making perfect Southern cornbread:

1. Good Southern corn meal.

2. Creamy, pourable batter—like thick pancake batter.

3. Hot cast iron cookware.

CORNBREAD'S BEST FRIEND— CAST IRON

The secret to great Southern cornbread is in the pan—a well-seasoned cast iron pan. Seasoning gives iron cookware its smooth, natural non-stick finish. It takes a little time and care, but good cornbread is worth it.

Whether your skillet or corn stick pans are new or just in need of a little attention, the following steps will get you baking right with cast iron:

WASH cookware thoroughly and dry it completely with a towel.

RUB it inside and out with vegetable oil or shortening.

HEAT the cookware upside down (to prevent the build-up of oil inside the pan) at 350°F. for one hour. Lay foil or a baking sheet on the rack below to catch any drips. Remove the pan from the oven and wipe with a paper towel. It's ready to use.

TO LOCK in the seasoning, fry bacon or sausage in your cast iron skillet whenever possible.

TO MAINTAIN the finish, clean cast iron after each use with hot water and a good stiff brush; never use harsh or abrasive detergents, and never put it in the dishwasher.

DRY thoroughly to protect it from rust.

GREASE cookware lightly before storing it.

Southern Cornbread

This is the benchmark recipe for Southern cornbread that has appeared on the Martha White bag for generations.

Prep Time: 10 minutes (Ready in 35 minutes)

1	**egg**
1⅓	**cups milk or 1¾ cups buttermilk**
¼	**cup oil or melted shortening**
2	**cups Martha White® Self-Rising Corn Meal Mix**

1. Heat oven to 450°F. Grease 9-inch cast iron skillet or 9-inch square pan; place in oven to heat.*

2. Meanwhile, in large bowl, beat egg. Add all remaining ingredients; mix well. (Batter should be creamy and pourable. If batter is too thick, add more liquid.) Pour batter into hot greased skillet.

3. Bake at 450°F. for 20 to 25 minutes or until golden brown.

Yield: 8 servings

TIP: * Recipe can be baked in muffin cups or cornbread stick pans. Grease 12 muffin cups or 16 cornbread stick pans. Bake at 450°F. for 15 to 20 minutes.

Southern Cornbread

Alison Krauss' Winning Cornbread

Prep Time: 30 minutes

1	tablespoon bacon drippings
¾	cup Martha White® Self-Rising Corn Meal Mix
¼	cup Martha White® Self-Rising Flour
1	tablespoon sugar
1	cup buttermilk*
3	tablespoons oil
1	egg, beaten
	Martha White® Corn Meal

1. Heat oven to 450°F. Grease 8-inch cast iron skillet with bacon drippings; place in oven to heat.

2. In large bowl, combine corn meal mix, flour and sugar; mix well. Add buttermilk, oil and egg; blend well. Sprinkle small amount of corn meal into hot greased skillet. Pour batter over corn meal in hot skillet.

3. Bake at 450°F. for 10 to 15 minutes or until golden brown.

Yield: 6 servings

TIP: * To substitute for buttermilk, use 1 tablespoon vinegar or lemon juice plus milk to make 1 cup.

Alison Krauss

From 1996 to 1998, Martha White Foods sponsored the tour of Grammy- and Country Music Association Award-winners, Alison Krauss & Union Station. The tour reached out to young bluegrass and country fans to promote the company's convenient baking mixes and flour and corn meal products.

Caramelized Sweet Onion Swiss Cornbread

Prep Time: 10 minutes (Ready in 35 minutes)

2	tablespoons butter or margarine
1	large onion, chopped
2	eggs
1⅓	cups milk or 1¾ cups buttermilk
2	cups Martha White® Self-Rising Corn Meal Mix
4	oz. (1 cup) shredded Swiss cheese

1. Heat oven to 450°F. Grease 9-inch cast iron skillet; place in oven to heat.

2. Melt butter in medium skillet over low heat. Add onion; cook about 15 minutes or until golden brown, stirring occasionally.

3. In medium bowl, beat eggs. Stir in milk. Add corn meal mix; stir until smooth. Stir in cheese and cooked onion. Pour batter into hot greased skillet.

4. Bake at 450°F. for 20 to 25 minutes or until golden brown.

Yield: 8 servings

Martha White Southern Sausage Cornbread

Prep Time: 10 minutes (Ready in 35 minutes)

- ½ **lb. bulk pork sausage**
- 1 **egg**
- 2 **cups Martha White® Self-Rising Corn Meal Mix**
- 1⅓ **cups milk or 1¾ cups buttermilk**
- ¼ **cup oil or melted shortening**

1. Heat oven to 450°F. In 10-inch cast iron skillet, cook sausage over medium heat until thoroughly cooked. Drain sausage; discard drippings from skillet. Place skillet in oven to heat.

2. In medium bowl, beat egg. Add corn meal mix, 1⅓ cups milk and oil; stir until smooth. Stir in sausage. (Batter should be pourable. If batter is too thick, add additional milk.) Pour batter into hot skillet.

3. Bake at 450°F. for 20 to 25 minutes or until golden brown.

Yield: 8 servings

Martha White Country-Style Cornbread

Omit the egg in cornbread batter and it bakes up dense and moist inside like this traditional favorite.

Prep Time: 10 minutes (Ready in 35 minutes)

- 2 **cups Martha White® Self-Rising Corn Meal Mix**
- 1¾ **cups buttermilk***
- ¼ **cup oil or melted shortening**

1. Heat oven to 450°F. Grease 9-inch cast iron skillet or 9-inch square pan; place in oven to heat.**

2. In large bowl, combine all ingredients; mix well. Pour batter into hot greased skillet.

3. Bake at 450°F. for 20 to 25 minutes or until golden brown.

Yield: 8 servings

TIPS: *To substitute for buttermilk, use 5 teaspoons vinegar or lemon juice plus milk to make 1¾ cups.

**Recipe can be baked in muffin cups or cornbread stick pans. Grease 12 muffin cups or 16 cornbread stick pans. Bake at 450°F. for 15 to 20 minutes.

Sour Cream and Onion Cornbread

Prep Time: 10 minutes (Ready in 45 minutes)

- 2 **tablespoons butter**
- ½ **cup chopped onion**
- 2 **(7.5-oz.) pkg. Martha White® Yellow Corn Muffin Mix**
- 1 **cup milk**
- 1 **(8-oz.) container sour cream**

1. Heat oven to 375°F. Grease bottom only of 9-inch square pan. Melt butter in small skillet. Add onion; cook and stir until tender.

2. In medium bowl, combine cooked onion and all remaining ingredients; mix well. Pour batter into greased pan.

3. Bake at 375°F. for 30 to 35 minutes or until golden brown.

Yield: 8 servings

Golden Cornbread

If you like cornbread that's yellow, cakey and sweet, this recipe is for you.

Prep Time: 10 minutes (Ready in 35 minutes)

- 1½ **cups Martha White® Self-Rising Corn Meal Mix**
- 1 **cup Martha White® All Purpose Flour**
- ¼ **cup sugar**
- 1 **cup milk**
- ¼ **cup oil or melted shortening**
- 2 **eggs, slightly beaten**

1. Heat oven to 450°F. Grease 8- or 9-inch square pan.* In large bowl, combine all ingredients; mix well. Pour batter into greased pan.

2. Bake at 450°F. for 20 to 25 minutes or until toothpick inserted in center comes out clean.

Yield: 8 servings

TIP: * Recipe can be baked in muffin cups or cornbread stick pans. Grease 12 muffin cups or 16 cornbread stick pans. Bake at 450°F. for 15 to 20 minutes.

Three Reasons Why Everyone Should Learn How to Make Really Good Cornbread

1. Cornbread is easy to make. Stir the batter up, pour it into a pan and bake.

2. Cornbread is the best accompaniment to beans and greens for sopping up the "pot likker."

3. Cornbread is an easy way to transform a simple meal into a rib-sticking dinner.

Crispy Bacon Dijon Mustard Cornbread

A little bacon is the easy way to achieve the traditional flavor of cracklings in cornbread.

Prep Time: 20 minutes (Ready in 45 minutes)

- 8 **slices bacon**
- 1½ **cups milk**
- ¼ **cup Dijon or prepared mustard**
- 1 **egg, beaten**
- 2 **cups Martha White® Self-Rising Corn Meal Mix**

1. Heat oven to 450°F. In 12-inch cast iron skillet, cook bacon over medium heat until crisp.

2. Meanwhile, in medium bowl, combine milk, mustard and egg; mix well. Add corn meal mix; blend well.

3. Remove bacon from skillet; drain on paper towels. Remove drippings from skillet; reserve. Crumble bacon; sprinkle evenly in skillet. Add 1 tablespoon reserved drippings to skillet. Stir 3 tablespoons reserved drippings into cornbread batter; blend well. Pour batter over bacon in skillet.

4. Bake at 450°F. for 20 to 25 minutes or until golden brown. Immediately remove from skillet; place on serving plate.

Yield: 8 servings

Crispy Bacon Dijon Mustard Cornbread

Cornbread Preferences

Sweet vs. Unsweet

White vs. Yellow Corn Meal

The debate rages on among cornbread lovers. For Southern purists, the sugar bowl doesn't come near the cornbread batter, and they prefer white corn meal. Residents in the Southwest prefer unsweetened cornbread made with yellow corn meal. And everywhere else, people like their cornbread yellow and sweet.

The Major Cornbread Regions at a Glance			
	Regions		
Ingredients	South	Southwest	Rest of U.S.
Corn Meal	White	Yellow	Yellow
Flour	None to Very Little	Some	Lots
Sugar	None to Very Little	None to Very Little	Lots
Pan	Cast Iron	Baking Pan	Baking Pan or Muffin Pan

Cornbread Preferences

Corn Light Bread with Pecans

An updated version of a Middle Tennessee favorite, corn light bread is a sweet, moist cornbread baked in a loaf pan.

Prep Time: 20 minutes
(Ready in 2 hours 40 minutes)

- 1½ **cups Martha White® Self-Rising Corn Meal Mix**
- ½ **cup Martha White® All Purpose Flour**
- ½ **cup sugar**
- ½ **cup chopped pecans**
- 1½ **cups buttermilk***
- ½ **cup butter or margarine, melted**

1. In medium bowl, combine all ingredients; stir well blended. Let stand 20 minutes.

2. Heat oven to 350°F. Grease bottom only of 8x4-inch loaf pan. Stir batter slightly; pour into greased pan.

3. Bake at 350°F. for 1 hour or until toothpick inserted in center comes out clean. Cool in pan 10 minutes. Invert bread onto wire rack; cool 1 hour or until completely cooled.

Yield: 10 servings

TIP: * To substitute for buttermilk, use 4½ teaspoons vinegar or lemon juice plus milk to make 1½ cups.

Corn Light Bread with Pecans

Martha White Corn Meal Glossary

WHITE OR YELLOW CORN MEAL

White corn meal (made from white corn) and yellow corn meal (made from yellow corn) have slightly different flavors. Personal preferences for each are often associated with the areas where white or yellow corn grows. Martha White corn meal is made from whole kernel corn including the sweet germ and bran. The sweet germ and corn oil provide the nutlike flavor of corn; the bran contributes the characteristic texture.

SELF-RISING CORN MEAL

Baking powder and salt have been blended with plain corn meal for convenient, fool-proof baking. Self-rising corn meal is available made with white or yellow corn.

SELF-RISING CORN MEAL MIX

This is the best selling Martha White corn meal product. The corn meal is blended with a small amount of flour and leavening for lighter, moister cornbread. It's available made with white or yellow corn.

BUTTERMILK SELF-RISING CORN MEAL MIX

Buttermilk powder, which gives a traditional tangy flavor to cornbread, is added to self-rising corn meal mix. This product is convenient for folks who don't keep fresh buttermilk on hand. It's available only made with white corn.

POUCH MIXES

For added convenience, Martha White cornbread pouch mixes are also available in a variety of flavors.

Classic Tex-Mex Cornbread Supreme

Prep Time: 20 minutes (Ready in 1 hour)

- 2 cups **Martha White® Self-Rising Corn Meal Mix**
- 1 cup **sour cream**
- ½ cup **milk**
- 1 **(8.5-oz.) can cream-style corn**
- 1 **(4.5-oz.) can chopped green chiles, drained**
- 4 oz. (1 cup) **shredded Cheddar cheese**
- 2 tablespoons **chopped jalapeño chiles**

1. Heat oven to 400°F. Grease 9-inch square pan. In large bowl, combine corn meal mix, sour cream and milk; blend well. Add all remaining ingredients; mix well. Pour batter into greased pan.

2. Bake at 400°F. for 40 minutes or until golden brown. Cool 10 minutes before serving.

Yield: 8 servings

Classic Corn Meal Waffles

Crispy waffles are a great choice for cornbread lovers who really love the crust. Serve these as you would cornbread.

Prep Time: 40 minutes

- 1½ cups **Martha White® Self-Rising Corn Meal Mix**
- 1¼ cups **milk**
- ¼ cup **oil or melted shortening**

1. Heat waffle iron. In medium bowl, combine corn meal mix, milk and oil; stir unto smooth.

2. For each waffle, pour batter into hot waffle iron. Bake until steaming stops and waffle is dark golden brown. If batter thickens, add additional milk.

Yield: 12 waffles

Classic Tex-Mex Cornbread Supreme and Classic Corn Meal Waffles

PASSING IT ON

When many women began working outside the home, the Martha White Kitchens took on the responsibility for helping young people learn Southern baking techniques that for generations had been passed down from mother to child. The company provided new convenience products and recipes for the changing times. To spread the word, Martha White home economists conducted cooking schools in communities all over the South for home economics students, homemaker groups and through the extension service. Today, millions of Martha White batter-spattered leaflets are treasured in recipe collections from Asheville to Vicksburg to Bowling Green. And a Martha White Foods sponsored 4-H program is teaching basic baking skills to a third generation of Southern bakers. As long as the Martha White recipes are here to provide guidance, the traditions of Southern baking will continue.

Linda Carman, Martha White® spokesperson, continues to encourage young 4-H participants, just as she did here in the 1980s.

Swiss Bacon Onion Cornbread

Prep Time: 30 minutes (Ready in 1 hour)

4	slices bacon
1	large onion, chopped
2	cups Martha White® Self-Rising Corn Meal Mix
6	oz. (1½ cups) shredded Swiss cheese
1⅓	cups milk
2	eggs, beaten

1. Heat oven to 425°F. Grease 13x9-inch pan. In large skillet, cook bacon over medium heat until crisp. Remove bacon from skillet; drain on paper towels. Crumble bacon. Reserve ¼ cup drippings in skillet. Add onion to reserved drippings; cook until tender, stirring occasionally.

2. In large bowl, combine corn meal mix, cheese, milk and eggs; stir until smooth. Stir in crumbled bacon and onion. Pour into greased pan.

3. Bake at 425°F. for 25 to 30 minutes or until golden brown.

Yield: 12 servings

Swiss Bacon Onion Cornbread

Sweet Milk Corn Cakes

Too hot to heat the oven? Corn cakes are the answer for enjoying cornbread—and a cool kitchen.

Prep Time: 20 minutes

- 1   egg
- ¾   cup milk
- 1   tablespoon oil
- 1   cup Martha White® Self-Rising Corn Meal Mix
- ½   teaspoon sugar

1. Heat griddle or large skillet to medium heat (350°F.). Grease lightly with oil. Griddle is ready when small drops of water sizzle and disappear almost immediately. Corn cakes will stick if griddle is too cool.

2. In large bowl, beat egg. Add all ingredients; mix well. If batter is too thick, add some additional milk.

3. For each corn cake, pour ¼ cup batter onto hot griddle. Cook until edges look cooked and bubbles begin to break on surface, turning once.

Yield: 6 corn cakes

Green Chile Corn Muffins

Prep Time: 30 minutes

- 2   (6-oz.) pkg. Martha White® Cotton Pickin' or Buttermilk Cornbread Mix
- 1   cup milk
- 1   egg, beaten
- 1   (4.5-oz.) can chopped green chiles, undrained
- 4   oz. (1 cup) shredded Monterey Jack cheese
- 1   jalapeño chile, chopped, if desired

1. Heat oven to 450°F. Grease 14 muffin cups or spray with nonstick cooking spray.

2. In large bowl, combine cornbread mix, milk and egg; stir until smooth. Stir in green chiles, cheese and jalapeño chile. Fill muffin cups ¾ full.

3. Bake at 450°F. for 15 to 20 minutes or until golden brown. Serve warm.

Yield: 14 muffins

Green Chile Corn Muffins

Hot Water Hoecakes

These old fashioned corn cakes, rich and flavorful, are fried until crispy and brown.

Prep Time: 20 minutes

> **Shortening**
> 1 **cup Martha White® Self-Rising Corn Meal Mix**
> 1¾ **cups boiling water**

1. In heavy skillet, heat ¼ inch shortening over medium heat to 375°F. In large bowl, combine corn meal mix and boiling water ; mix well.

2. For each corn cake, pour heaping tablespoonful batter into hot shortening. Cook until golden brown, turning once. Serve warm.

Yield: 20 corn cakes

Mexi Corn Cakes

Prep Time: 15 minutes

> 1 **(6-oz.) pkg. Martha White® Cotton Pickin' or Buttermilk Cornbread Mix**
> ⅔ **cup milk**
> 1 **egg, beaten**
> 1 **(11-oz.) can vacuum-packed whole kernel corn with red and green peppers, drained**
> ¼ **teaspoon garlic salt**

1. Heat griddle or large skillet to medium heat (350°F.). Grease lightly with oil. Griddle is ready when small drops of water sizzle and disappear almost immediately. Corn cakes will stick if griddle is too cool.

2. In medium bowl, combine cornbread mix, milk and egg; blend well. Stir in corn and garlic salt.

3. For each corn cake, pour ¼ cup batter onto hot griddle. Cook until deep golden brown on both sides, turning once.

Yield: 10 corn cakes

Hush Puppies

Traditionally, hush puppies are really just fried cornbread cooked in hot fat after frying fish. They're a must with crispy catfish and slaw.

Prep Time: 20 minutes

> **Oil for deep frying**
> 2 **cups Martha White® Self-Rising Corn Meal Mix**
> 3 **tablespoons Martha White® Self-Rising Flour**
> 1 **to 2 tablespoons finely chopped onion**
> 1 **cup milk or water**
> 1 **egg, beaten**

1. In deep fryer or heavy skillet, heat 2 to 3 inches oil over medium heat to 375°F. In large bowl, combine corn meal mix, flour and onion; mix well. Add milk and egg; mix well. Let stand 5 minutes.

2. Drop batter by tablespoonfuls into hot oil. Fry until golden brown, turning several times. Drain on paper towels. Serve warm.

Yield: 16 hush puppies

Breakfast, the South's Favorite Meal

Pass the Biscuits

Many Southerners proudly declare that breakfast is their favorite meal, and some eat biscuits and scrambled eggs for supper. A hearty breakfast was once a daily necessity for farmers, but it now has become an anticipated weekend feast, complete with biscuits, grits, eggs, fried apples and country ham, sausage or bacon—and, of course, gravy, preserves and sorghum.

Making Biscuits

The advent of commercially produced baking powder and baking soda changed Southern baking forever. That's when biscuits joined cornbread at the head of the table. Soon came self-rising flour, the South's first convenience mix and the one that made Martha White flour famous. Self-Rising Flour with Hot Rize® streamlined daily biscuit-making by blending the flour with just the right amount of baking powder and salt for perfect biscuits every time. It didn't take long for Southerners to refer to self-rising flour simply as "biscuit flour."

Sorghum and Cane Syrup

In the rural South, syrups made from sorghum or sugar cane were traditional sweeteners for biscuits, pancakes and cornbread. Many families even grew their own sorghum or cane. Home-pressed syrup may almost be a thing of the past, but it remains a seriously sweet favorite in the South.

Country Ham

Country ham is another legacy of self-sufficient Southern farmers. Country hams are salted, smoked and cured for almost a year. What began as a preservation technique is now a revered art form.

Martha White Hot Rize® Biscuits, page 9

Muffins
& Quick Loaves

"Want something to eat?" is the familiar greeting heard in kitchens across the South. It's common courtesy to offer a little something with a cup of coffee or to send a batch of muffins home with a neighbor. Whether it's a loaf of banana bread cooling on the kitchen counter or muffins hot from the oven, stir-up-and-bake breads are nice to have on hand.

French Cinnamon Muffins, page 42

French Cinnamon Muffins

Prep Time: 20 minutes (Ready in 40 minutes)

  2 **cups Martha White® Self-Rising Flour**
  ½ **cup sugar**
  ¼ **teaspoon cinnamon**
  ⅔ **cup milk**
  ⅓ **cup butter or margarine, melted, cooled**
  1 **egg**
  ¼ **cup sugar**
  1 **teaspoon cinnamon**
  ¼ **cup butter or margarine, melted**

1. Heat oven to 425°F. Grease 12 muffin cups or line with paper baking cups. In large bowl, combine flour, ½ cup sugar and ¼ teaspoon cinnamon; mix well.

2. In small bowl, combine milk, ⅓ cup melted butter and egg; blend well. Add to flour mixture; stir just until dry ingredients are moistened. (Batter will be slightly lumpy.) Fill greased muffin cups ⅔ full.

3. Bake at 425°F. for 15 to 18 minutes or until golden brown.

4. Meanwhile, in small bowl, combine ¼ cup sugar and 1 teaspoon cinnamon; mix well.

5. Remove muffins from muffin cups. Dip tops of warm muffins in ¼ cup melted butter; dip in sugar-cinnamon mixture. Serve warm.

Yield: 12 muffins

Classic Muffins

Prep Time: 30 minutes

  2 **cups Martha White® Self-Rising Flour**
  ¼ **cup sugar**
  1 **cup milk**
  3 **tablespoons oil**
  1 **egg**

1. Heat oven to 425°F. Grease 12 muffin cups. In medium bowl, combine flour and sugar; mix well.

2. In small bowl, combine milk, oil and egg; blend well. Add to flour mixture; stir just until dry ingredients are moistened. (Batter will be slightly lumpy.) Fill greased muffin cups ⅔ full.

3. Bake at 425°F. for 18 to 20 minutes or until golden brown. Serve warm.

Yield: 12 muffins

Homemade Blueberry Muffins

Prep Time: 30 minutes

2	cups Martha White® Self-Rising Flour
½	cup sugar
⅔	cup milk
⅓	cup butter or margarine, melted, cooled
1	egg
1	cup fresh blueberries*

1. Heat oven to 425°F. Grease 12 muffin cups. In large bowl, combine flour and sugar; mix well.

2. In small bowl, combine milk, melted butter and egg; blend well. Add to flour mixture; stir just until dry ingredients are moistened. (Batter will be slightly lumpy.) Gently fold in blueberries. Fill greased muffin cups ⅔ full.

3. Bake at 425°F. for 15 to 18 minutes or until golden brown. Serve warm.

Yield: 12 muffins

TIP: * One cup canned blueberries, rinsed and drained or 1 cup frozen blueberries, thawed and drained, can be substituted for the fresh blueberries.

Applesauce-Spice Muffins

Prep Time: 30 minutes

2	cups Martha White® Self-Rising Flour
⅓	cup sugar
½	teaspoon cinnamon
¼	teaspoon nutmeg
1	cup applesauce
½	cup milk
3	tablespoons oil
1	egg

1. Heat oven to 425°F. Grease 12 muffin cups. In large bowl, combine flour, sugar, cinnamon and nutmeg; mix well.

2. In small bowl, combine applesauce, milk, oil and egg; blend well. Add to flour mixture; stir just until dry ingredients are moistened. (Batter will be slightly lumpy.) Fill greased muffin cups ⅔ full.

3. Bake at 425°F. for 18 to 20 minutes or until golden brown. Serve warm.

Yield: 12 muffins

Martha's Muffin Method

Homemade muffins are the quickest of the quick breads. Using self-rising flour simplifies the stir-and-bake batter, and the muffins bake in minutes. Follow this classic three-step method, and you can enjoy home-baked muffins anytime.

1. Mix the dry: Combine all the dry ingredients in a bowl.

2. Mix the wet: Combine all the liquid ingredients in another bowl.

3. Mix the wet into the dry: Add the liquid to the dry ingredients and stir just until moistened.

Frosty Orange Muffins

Frosty Orange Muffins

These muffins can be whatever you want them to be. Kids think they're cupcakes with luscious frosting; adults think they're a sophisticated snack.

Prep Time: 20 minutes (Ready in 40 minutes)

MUFFINS
- 2 **cups Martha White® Self-Rising Flour**
- 1/3 **cup sugar**
- 1 **tablespoon grated orange peel**
- 3/4 **cup orange juice**
- 1/4 **cup oil**
- 1 **egg**

TOPPING
- 1 **(3-oz.) pkg. cream cheese, softened**
- 1/4 **cup powdered sugar**
- 1 **teaspoon grated orange peel**

1. Heat oven to 400°F. Grease 12 muffin cups. In medium bowl, combine flour, sugar and 1 tablespoon orange peel; mix well.

2. In small bowl, combine orange juice, oil and egg; blend well. Add to flour mixture; stir just until dry ingredients are moistened. (Batter will be slightly lumpy.) Fill greased muffin cups 2/3 full.

3. Bake at 400°F. for 18 to 20 minutes or until golden brown.

4. Meanwhile, combine all topping ingredients; blend well.

5. Remove muffins from muffin cups. Cool 10 minutes. Spread each muffin with topping. Serve warm. Store in refrigerator.

Yield: 12 muffins

Apricot Muffins

Use kitchen scissors for an easy way to cut up the dried fruit.

Prep Time: 30 minutes
- 2 **cups Martha White® Self-Rising Flour**
- 1/2 **cup sugar**
- 1/2 **cup chopped dried apricots**
- 2/3 **cup milk**
- 1/3 **cup butter or margarine, melted, cooled**
- 1/2 **teaspoon vanilla**
- 1 **egg**

1. Heat oven to 425°F. Grease 12 muffin cups. In medium bowl, combine flour and sugar; mix well. Stir in apricots.

2. In medium bowl, combine milk, melted butter, vanilla and egg; blend well. Add to flour mixture; stir just until dry ingredients are moistened. (Batter will be slightly lumpy.) Fill greased muffin cups 2/3 full.

3. Bake at 425°F. for 15 to 18 minutes or until golden brown. Serve warm.

Yield: 12 muffins

Strawberry Banana Nut Muffins

Prep Time: 30 minutes

1	(7-oz.) pkg. Martha White® Strawberry Muffin Mix
½	cup chopped walnuts
⅓	cup milk
½	cup mashed ripe banana

1. Heat oven to 425°F. Grease 6 muffin cups. In small bowl, combine muffin mix and walnuts; mix well.

2. Add milk; stir just until dry ingredients are moistened. Stir in banana. Fill greased muffin cups ⅔ full.

3. Bake at 425°F. for 12 to 14 minutes or until golden brown. Serve warm.

Yield: 6 muffins

Cheese Danish Muffins

A simple cream-cheese mixture creates a cheesecake-like layer as the muffins bake.

Prep Time: 30 minutes

2	(3-oz.) pkg. cream cheese, softened
3	tablespoons sugar
1	egg
2	(7-oz.) pkg. Martha White® Muffin Mix, any fruit flavor
1	cup milk

1. Heat oven to 425°F. Grease 12 muffin cups. In large bowl, combine cream cheese and sugar; beat until smooth. Add egg; beat well.

2. In medium bowl, combine muffin mix and milk; stir just until dry ingredients are moistened. Fill greased muffin cups ⅔ full. Top each muffin with about 1 tablespoon cream cheese mixture.

3. Bake at 425°F. for 12 to 15 minutes or until cream cheese is set. Serve warm. Store in refrigerator.

Yield: 12 muffins

Easy Date Nut Muffins

Prep Time: 30 minutes

1	(7-oz.) pkg. Martha White® Apple Cinnamon Muffin Mix
½	cup chopped dates
½	cup chopped pecans
½	cup milk

1. Heat oven to 400°F. Grease 6 muffin cups. In large bowl, combine all ingredients; stir just until dry ingredients are moistened. Fill greased muffin cups ⅔ full.

2. Bake at 400°F. for 15 to 18 minutes or until golden brown. Serve warm.

Yield: 6 muffins

Molasses Bran Muffins

Prep Time: 30 minutes

2	cups shreds of whole bran cereal
1½	cups milk
¼	cup molasses
¼	cup shortening
1	egg
1½	cups Martha White® All Purpose Flour
½	cup sugar
1½	teaspoons baking soda
½	teaspoon salt
½	cup raisins

1. Heat oven to 400° F. Line with paper baking cups or grease 18 muffin cups. In medium bowl, combine cereal, milk and molasses; mix well. Let stand 1 to 2 minutes until cereal is softened. Add shortening and egg; beat well.

2. In large bowl, combine flour, sugar, baking soda and salt; mix well. Stir in raisins. Add cereal mixture all at once to flour mixture; stir just until dry ingredients are moistened. Divide batter evenly into paper-lined muffin cups.

3. Bake at 400°F. for 14 to 18 minutes or until toothpick inserted in center comes out clean. Immediately remove from pan. Serve warm.

Yield: 18 muffins

Refrigerator Bran Muffins

Prep Time: 15 minutes (Ready in 40 minutes)

2½	cups buttermilk*
⅓	cup oil
2	eggs
3	cups bran flakes cereal with or without raisins
2½	cups Martha White® Self-Rising Flour
1	cup sugar

1. In large bowl, combine buttermilk, oil and eggs; beat well. Add all remaining ingredients; stir just until dry ingredients are moistened. Batter can be baked immediately or stored for up to 2 weeks in tightly covered container in refrigerator.

2. When ready to bake, heat oven to 400°F. Line desired number of muffin cups with paper baking cups. Stir batter. Fill paper-lined muffin cups ⅔ full.

3. Bake at 400°F. for 20 to 25 minutes or until toothpick inserted in center comes out clean. Immediately remove from muffin cups. Serve warm.

Yield: 30 muffins

TIP: * To substitute for buttermilk, use 2 tablespoons plus 1½ teaspoons vinegar or lemon juice plus milk to make 2½ cups.

Butter Pecan Muffins

Brown sugar and real butter give these muffins a rich caramel flavor, which complements the pecans.

Prep Time: 30 minutes

- 1½ **cups Martha White® Self-Rising Flour**
- 1 **cup chopped pecans**
- ½ **cup firmly packed brown sugar**
- ¾ **cup milk**
- ¼ **cup butter or margarine, melted, cooled**
- ½ **teaspoon vanilla**
- 1 **egg, beaten**

1. Heat oven to 400°F. Grease 10 muffin cups. In large bowl, combine flour, pecans and brown sugar; mix well.

2. In small bowl, combine milk, butter, vanilla and egg; blend well. Add to flour mixture; stir just until dry ingredients are moistened. Fill greased muffin cups ⅔ full.

3. Bake at 400°F. for 15 minutes or until golden brown. Serve warm.

Yield: 10 muffins

Pumpkin Streusel Muffins

Prep Time: 20 minutes (Ready in 45 minutes)

MUFFINS
- ½ **cup milk**
- ½ **cup canned pumpkin**
- ⅓ **cup oil**
- 1 **egg, beaten**
- 1¾ **cups Martha White® Self-Rising Flour**
- ½ **cup sugar**
- ½ **teaspoon cinnamon**
- ¼ **teaspoon nutmeg**
- 1 **(3-oz.) pkg. cream cheese**

TOPPING
- ¼ **cup firmly packed brown sugar**
- ½ **teaspoon cinnamon**
- 1 **tablespoon butter or margarine**
- ¼ **cup finely chopped nuts**

1. Heat oven to 400°F. Grease bottoms only of 12 muffin cups or line with paper baking cups. In medium bowl, combine milk, pumpkin, oil and egg; blend well.

2. Add flour, sugar, ½ teaspoon cinnamon and nutmeg; stir just until dry ingredients are moistened. (Batter will be lumpy.) Fill greased muffin cups ½ full, reserving remaining batter.

3. Divide cream cheese into 12 equal pieces. Place 1 piece on batter in each cup. Top with reserved batter, filling each cup about ¾ full. In small bowl, combine all topping ingredients; mix well. Sprinkle evenly over each muffin.

4. Bake at 400°F. for 18 to 22 minutes or until golden brown. Immediately remove from muffin cups. Serve warm. Store in refrigerator.

Yield: 12 muffins

Flatt and Scruggs

Lester Flatt, Earl Scruggs and the Foggy Mountain Boys became bluegrass music legends with the help of Martha White Foods. In 1953, the company hired the then-unknown band to barnstorm through the South promoting its flour and corn meal. They became known as the "World's Greatest Flour Peddlers," appearing on the Grand Ole Opry, playing on the "Martha White Biscuit and Cornbread Time" radio show and hosting the "Flatt and Scruggs" television program. Singer Lester Flatt, and Earl Scruggs, known as the fastest banjo-picker in the world, performed twice at Carnegie Hall; played the Hollywood Bowl; recorded the theme song for "The Beverly Hillbillies" television show; and appeared on that show six times.

A MESSAGE FROM OUR SPONSOR

Flatt and Scruggs opened the Martha White portion of the Grand Ole Opry every Saturday night by singing "You Bake Right with Martha White." The jingle quickly became one of Flatt and Scruggs' most-requested songs—even at New York City's Carnegie Hall. Today, it's a bluegrass standard. In the 1960s, popular bluegrass musicians Jim and Jesse McReynolds also helped spread the word for Martha White products. Lester Flatt formed the Nashville Grass and continued on with Martha White Foods into the early 1970s. Country music star Marty Stuart got his start with the band and came to national attention

at the young age of 13. The bluegrass tradition continued 25 years later with the Martha White Foods tour sponsorship of young bluegrass sensation Alison Krauss and Union Station.

Today, the Country Music Foundation and the International Bluegrass Music Association regard Martha White Foods as a respected patron fostering the growth and popularity of this uniquely American music.

Flatt and Scruggs and the Foggy Mountain Boys with the "Martha White Express" in 1955.

Peppery Cheese Muffins

Corn muffins become contemporary with the addition of a little Parmesan cheese and black pepper.

Prep Time: 30 minutes

- 1 **cup buttermilk***
- 2 **tablespoons butter or margarine, melted**
- 2 **eggs**
- 1 **cup Martha White® Self-Rising Corn Meal Mix**
- ¾ **cup Martha White® Self-Rising Flour**
- ½ **cup grated Parmesan cheese**
- 1½ **teaspoons pepper**

1. Heat oven to 450°F. Grease 12 muffin cups. In medium bowl, combine buttermilk, melted butter and eggs; blend well.

2. Add corn meal mix, flour, cheese and pepper; mix well. Fill greased muffin cups ¾ full.

3. Bake at 450°F. for 18 to 20 minutes or until golden brown. Serve warm.

Yield: 12 muffins

TIP: * To substitute for buttermilk, use 1 tablespoon vinegar or lemon juice plus milk to make 1 cup.

Parmesan Fresh Herb Muffins

Prep Time: 30 minutes

- 1 **cup Martha White® Self-Rising Flour**
- 1 **cup Martha White® Self-Rising Corn Meal Mix**
- 1½ **cups buttermilk***
- ¼ **cup butter or margarine, melted**
- 2 **eggs, beaten**
- ½ **cup grated Parmesan cheese**
- ⅓ **cup chopped fresh basil, dill and/or parsley**
- ½ **teaspoon cracked black pepper**

1. Heat oven to 450°F. Grease 14 muffin cups. In medium bowl, combine flour and corn meal mix; mix well.

2. Add buttermilk, butter and eggs; blend well. Add all remaining ingredients; stir just until blended. Fill greased muffin cups ⅔ full.

3. Bake at 450°F. for 18 to 20 minutes or until golden brown. Serve warm.

Yield: 14 muffins

TIP: * To substitute for buttermilk, use 4½ teaspoons vinegar or lemon juice plus milk to make 1½ cups.

Parmesan Fresh Herb Muffins

Lemon Chive Pepper Muffins

Prep Time: 15 minutes (Ready in 35 minutes)

2	cups Martha White® Self-Rising Flour
½	cup sugar
¼	cup chopped fresh chives
1	tablespoon grated lemon peel
½	to 1 teaspoon coarse ground black pepper
¾	cup milk
⅓	cup oil
1	egg, slightly beaten

1. Heat oven to 400°F. Grease bottoms only of 12 muffin cups or line with paper baking cups. In medium bowl, combine flour, sugar, chives, lemon peel and pepper; mix well.

2. Add milk, oil and egg; stir just until dry ingredients are moistened. Fill greased muffin cups ¾ full.

3. Bake at 400°F. for 15 to 20 minutes or until light golden brown and toothpick inserted in center comes out clean. Serve warm.

Yield: 12 muffins

Cheddar Cheese Muffins

Prep Time: 30 minutes

2	cups Martha White® Self-Rising Flour
4	oz. (1 cup) finely shredded sharp Cheddar cheese
1	teaspoon dry mustard
½	teaspoon chili powder
1	cup milk
¼	cup oil
1	egg

1. Heat oven to 425°F. Grease 12 muffin cups. In large bowl, combine flour, cheese, dry mustard and chili powder; mix well.

2. In medium bowl, combine milk, oil and egg; beat well. Add to flour mixture; stir just until dry ingredients are moistened. (Batter will be slightly lumpy.) Spoon batter into greased muffin cups.

3. Bake at 425°F. for 18 to 20 minutes or until golden brown. Serve warm.

Yield: 12 muffins

And now, a message from our sponsor

You Bake Right with Martha White

Martha White Foods, Inc., Nashville, Tennessee

Cornbread Lyrics:

Now you bake right (uh-huh) with Martha White (Yes Ma'am)
Goodness gracious, good and light, Martha White
For the finest cornbread you can bake
Get Martha White Self-Rising Meal, Hot Rize® Self-Rising Meal.
Martha White Self-Rising Meal for goodness sake.

The famous Martha White advertising jingle was written in the early 1950s by the late Pat Twitty of Nashville. The song was made famous by legendary bluegrass musicians and Martha White spokesmen Lester Flatt and Earl Scruggs. Versions of the lyrics, such as the Cornbread Lyrics, have been adapted to promote the company's flagship products. Today, the song is a popular bluegrass music standard.

Zucchini Nut Bread

Prep Time: 20 minutes
(Ready in 2 hours 35 minutes)

- 2 cups Martha White® All Purpose Flour
- 1 cup sugar
- 2 teaspoons baking powder
- 1 teaspoon salt
- 3 teaspoons cinnamon
- 3 eggs
- 2 cups grated unpeeled zucchini (about 1 large)
- ¾ cup oil
- 1 tablespoon vanilla
- 1 cup chopped walnuts

1. Heat oven to 325°F. Grease and flour 9x5-inch loaf pan. In large bowl, combine flour, sugar, baking powder, salt and cinnamon; mix well.

2. In small bowl, beat eggs. Add zucchini, oil and vanilla; blend well. Add to flour mixture; stir just until dry ingredients are moistened. Gently fold in walnuts. Pour batter into greased and floured pan.

3. Bake at 325°F. for 60 to 65 minutes or until toothpick inserted in center comes out clean. Cool in pan 10 minutes. Remove from pan; place on wire rack. Cool 1 hour or until completely cooled. Wrap tightly and store in refrigerator.

Yield: 1 (12-slice) loaf

Strawberry Bread

Prep Time: 20 minutes
(Ready in 2 hours 55 minutes)

- ½ cup sugar
- ½ cup butter or margarine, softened
- 2 eggs
- 1 teaspoon vanilla
- 2 cups Martha White® All Purpose Flour
- ½ teaspoon salt
- ¼ teaspoon baking soda
- 1 cup strawberry preserves
- ½ cup buttermilk*
- ½ cup chopped pecans

1. Heat oven to 325°F. Grease bottom only of 8x4-inch loaf pan. In large bowl, combine sugar and butter; beat until light and fluffy. Add eggs 1 at a time, beating well after each addition. Stir in vanilla.

2. In medium bowl, combine flour, salt and baking soda; mix well. In small bowl, combine preserves and buttermilk; blend well. Add flour mixture alternately with preserves mixture to butter mixture, beginning and ending with flour mixture. Gently fold in pecans. Pour batter into greased pan.

3. Bake at 325°F. for 1 hour 20 minutes or until toothpick inserted in center comes out clean. Cool in pan 15 minutes. Remove from pan; place on wire rack. Cool 1 hour or until completely cooled. Wrap tightly and store in refrigerator.

Yield: 1 (12-slice) loaf

TIP: * To substitute for buttermilk, use 1½ teaspoons vinegar or lemon juice plus milk to make ½ cup.

Aunt Lois' Banana Nut Bread

Folks love this recipe—it's a longtime Martha White Kitchen favorite for snacking and giving.

Prep Time: 15 minutes (Ready in 2 hours)

1½	**cups Martha White® All Purpose Flour**
¾	**teaspoon baking soda**
¼	**teaspoon salt**
1	**cup sugar**
¾	**cup oil**
3	**tablespoons buttermilk***
2	**eggs, beaten**
1	**cup mashed ripe bananas**
½	**cup chopped pecans**

1. Heat oven to 325°F. Grease and flour bottom only of 8x4 or 9x5-inch loaf pan. In large bowl, combine flour, baking soda and salt; mix well.

2. Add sugar, oil, buttermilk and eggs; blend well. Add bananas and pecans; mix well. Pour batter into greased and floured pan.

3. Bake at 325°F. for 1¼ to 1½ hours or until toothpick inserted in center comes out clean. Cool in pan 15 minutes. Remove from pan; place on wire rack. Cool 1 hour or until completely cooled. Wrap tightly and store in refrigerator.

Yield: 1 (12-slice) loaf

TIP: * To substitute for buttermilk, use ½ teaspoon vinegar or lemon juice plus milk to make 3 tablespoons.

Spicy Apple Bread

Prep Time: 15 minutes
(Ready in 2 hours, 25 minutes)

1	**cup shreds of whole bran cereal**
1	**cup milk**
¾	**cup sugar**
½	**cup margarine or butter, softened**
2	**eggs**
1½	**cups Martha White® All Purpose Flour**
3	**teaspoons baking powder**
½	**teaspoon salt**
½	**teaspoon cinnamon**
¼	**teaspoon allspice**
¼	**teaspoon nutmeg**
1	**cup finely chopped, peeled apples**

1. Heat oven to 375° F. Grease bottom only of 8x4 or 9x5-inch loaf pan. In small bowl, combine cereal and milk; mix well. Let stand 5 minutes.

2. In large bowl, combine sugar and margarine; beat until light and fluffy. Add eggs and cereal mixture; beat well. Add flour, baking powder, salt, cinnamon, allspice and nutmeg; mix well. Fold in apples. Pour batter into greased pan.

3. Bake at 375° F. for 50 to 60 minutes or until toothpick inserted in center comes out clean. Cool 10 minutes. Remove from pan. Cool 1 hour or until completely cooled. Wrap tightly and store in refrigerator.

Yield: 1 (16-slice) loaf

Sweet Potatoes

Folks in the South love sweet potatoes. Any way you can fix them—baked, boiled, candied and mashed—they turn up in everything from biscuits to pies.

Nothing could be easier to prepare. Simply wash the potatoes and either boil or bake them right in their jackets.

TO BOIL: Cover the whole potatoes with water. Bring the water to a boil. Cover and simmer them until tender. The jackets will peel right off when the potatoes are cool enough to handle.

TO BAKE: Pierce the potato jacket in several places. Rub with oil if you prefer a soft skin. Place on a baking sheet and bake uncovered at 450° F. until soft.

Freezing Quick Breads

Most quick bread loaves freeze well, giving you a head start on holiday baking or a hearty treat during hectic weeks. Cool loaves completely; do not glaze or decorate. Wrap them tightly in plastic wrap, plastic bags or foil. Or, wrap individual slices separately, allowing them to thaw more quickly. Be sure to label the outside wrapping with the type of bread and the date. For optimum flavor, use within one month. To serve, slightly unwrap the bread and thaw at room temperature; glaze or decorate according to the recipe.

Southern Sweet Potato Bread

Great for gift-giving, snacking or breakfast on the run, this moist, lightly spiced loaf is studded with golden raisins and pecans. Cooked and mashed fresh sweet potatoes taste the best, but canned will work just fine.

Prep Time: 10 minutes
(Ready in 2 hours 25 minutes)

1½	cups **Martha White® Self-Rising Flour**
1	cup sugar
1	teaspoon nutmeg
½	teaspoon cinnamon
½	cup oil
2	tablespoons milk
2	eggs, slightly beaten
1	cup mashed cooked sweet potatoes
1	cup chopped pecans
½	cup golden raisins

1. Heat oven to 350°F. Grease bottom only of 8x4-inch loaf pan. In large bowl, combine flour, sugar, nutmeg and cinnamon; mix well.

2. Add oil, milk and eggs; blend well. Add sweet potatoes, pecans and raisins; mix well. Pour into greased pan.

3. Bake at 350°F. for 1¼ hours or until toothpick inserted in center comes out clean. Cool in pan 15 minutes. Remove from pan; place on wire rack. Cool 1 hour or until completely cooled. Wrap tightly and store in refrigerator.

Yield: 1 (12-slice) loaf

Southern Sweet Potato Bread

Lemon Poppy Seed Loaf

Prep Time: 20 minutes
(Ready in 1 hour 10 minutes)

2   (7.6-oz.) pkg. Martha White® Lemon
    Poppy Seed Muffin Mix
⅔   cup milk
¼   cup oil
2   eggs, beaten

1. Heat oven to 350°F. Grease bottom only of 9x5-inch loaf pan. In large bowl, combine all ingredients; mix well. Pour into greased pan.

2. Bake at 350°F. for 45 to 50 minutes or until toothpick inserted in center comes out clean. Cool in pan 10 minutes. Remove from pan; place on wire rack. Cool 1 hour or until completely cooled. Wrap tightly and store in refrigerator.

Yield: 1 (12-slice) loaf

Savory Swiss Olive Bread

Quick loaves don't have to be sweet. This one, flavored with Swiss cheese and ripe olives, makes a stylish appetizer or a great accent for a simple supper.

Prep Time: 10 minutes
(Ready in 2 hours 15 minutes)

2   cups Martha White® Self-Rising Flour
¼   teaspoon garlic powder
¾   cup milk
½   cup butter or margarine, melted
2   eggs
6   oz. (1½ cups) shredded Swiss or
    Cheddar cheese
1   (3.8-oz.) can sliced ripe olives, drained

1. Heat oven to 350°F. Grease bottom only of 8x4- or 9x5-inch loaf pan. In large bowl, combine flour and garlic powder; mix well.

2. In small bowl, combine milk, butter and eggs; blend well. Add to flour mixture; stir just until dry ingredients are moistened. Stir in cheese and olives. Pour into greased pan.

3. Bake at 350°F. for 50 to 55 minutes or until toothpick inserted in center comes out clean. Cool in pan 10 minutes. Remove from pan; place on wire rack. Cool 1 hour or until completely cooled. Wrap tightly and store in refrigerator.

Yield: 1 (12-slice) loaf

Savory Swiss Olive Bread

Peppery Pimiento Cheese Bread

Cheddar Cheese Bread

The Peppery Pimiento Cheese Bread variation tastes just like the favorite Southern sandwich spread.

Prep Time: 10 minutes
(Ready in 2 hours 15 minutes)

BREAD
- 2 **cups Martha White® Self-Rising Flour**
- 2 **teaspoons dry mustard**
- ¾ **cup milk**
- ½ **cup butter or margarine, melted**
- 2 **eggs**
- 4 **oz. (1 cup) shredded sharp Cheddar cheese**

TOPPING
- 1 **oz. (¼ cup) shredded sharp Cheddar cheese**
- 1 **tablespoon butter or margarine, cut into pieces**

1. Heat oven to 350°F. Grease bottom only of 8x4- or 9x5-inch loaf pan. In large bowl, combine flour and dry mustard; mix well.

2. In small bowl, combine milk, melted butter and eggs; blend well. Add to flour mixture; mix well. Stir in 1 cup cheese. Pour batter into greased pan. Sprinkle with ¼ cup cheese. Top with 1 tablespoon butter.

3. Bake at 350°F. for 50 to 55 minutes or until toothpick inserted in center comes out clean. Cool in pan 10 minutes. Remove from pan; place on wire rack. Cool 1 hour or until completely cooled. Wrap tightly and store in refrigerator.

Yield: 1 (12-slice) loaf

PEPPERY PIMIENTO CHEESE BREAD: Omit dry mustard. Stir in ½ teaspoon cracked black pepper and ½ cup chopped drained pimientos.

Cheesy Breadsticks

Prep Time: 45 minutes

- 1 **(5.5-oz.) pkg. Martha White® Bix Mix Buttermilk Biscuit Mix**
- ⅓ **cup milk**
- 4 **oz. (1 cup) shredded sharp Cheddar cheese**
- 1 **teaspoon dry mustard**
- ¼ **teaspoon crushed red pepper flakes, if desired**
- ¼ **cup butter or margarine, melted**
- 1 **egg, slightly beaten**

1. Heat oven to 375°F. Grease 13x9-inch pan. In large bowl, combine biscuit mix and milk; stir until smooth.

2. Add all remaining ingredients; mix well. Spread dough evenly in greased pan.

3. Bake at 375°F. for 15 to 20 minutes or until golden brown. Cool in pan 10 minutes. To serve, cut into 3x¾-inch strips.

Yield: 36 breadsticks

Country Soda Bread

Akin to Irish soda bread, this loaf is dense and chewy on the outside and tender on the inside. Serve it thinly sliced with cheese as an appetizer or as an accompaniment to soup or salad.

Prep Time: 10 minutes (Ready in 45 minutes)

- 3 cups Martha White® All Purpose Flour
- 1 cup Martha White® Self-Rising Corn Meal Mix
- 1 teaspoon baking soda
- 1½ cups buttermilk*

1. Heat oven to 425°F. Grease cookie sheet. In large bowl, combine flour, corn meal mix and baking soda; mix well. Add buttermilk; stir with fork just until soft dough forms. If dough seems too soft or too dry, add small amount of flour or buttermilk.

2. On lightly floured surface, knead dough gently about 10 times or until smooth. Shape into flat round loaf about 8 inches in diameter. Place on greased cookie sheet. With sharp knife, cut cross in top of loaf.

3. Bake at 425°F. for 30 to 35 minutes or until golden brown. Serve warm.

Yield: 1 (16-slice) loaf

TIP: * To substitute for buttermilk, use 4½ teaspoons vinegar or lemon juice plus milk to make 1½ cups.

Onion Flat Bread

Prep Time: 15 minutes
(Ready in 1 hour 5 minutes)

- 2 tablespoons butter or margarine
- 1 cup chopped onions
- 2 (6.5-oz.) pkg. Martha White® Pizza Crust Mix
- 1 cup hot water
- 1 tablespoon olive oil
- 1 teaspoon dried parsley flakes
  Salt and pepper

1. Heat oven to 450°F. Grease large cookie sheet. Melt butter in large skillet. Add onions; cook and stir until tender and translucent but not brown.

2. In large bowl, combine pizza crust mix, water and half of cooked onions; stir vigorously with spoon about 20 strokes to form a soft dough. With oiled hands, shape dough into smooth ball. Place dough on greased cookie sheet; press into 13x10-inch rectangle.

3. Spread dough with oil; top with remaining half of onions. Sprinkle with parsley. Add salt and pepper to taste. Let rise in warm place (80 to 85°F.) for 30 minutes or until dough has risen slightly.

4. Bake at 450°F. for 17 to 20 minutes or until golden brown. Serve warm.

Yield: 12 servings

Onion Flat Bread

Pancakes & Coffee cake

Cooking up a big pancake breakfast or offering a piece of warm coffee cake to the bleary-eyed can turn any Saturday into a special occasion. In today's busy world, families take advantage of the time they have together—and what better way than around the breakfast table. Starting the day with a good meal makes for good conversation and a good time.

Upside-Down Peach Coffee Cake, page 71

Easy Buttermilk Pancakes

These pancakes are a breeze to make with self-rising flour and buttermilk.

Prep Time: 20 minutes

2	eggs
2	cups buttermilk*
¼	cup oil
1¾	cups Martha White® Self-Rising Flour
2	tablespoons sugar
½	teaspoon baking soda
½	teaspoon salt

1. Heat griddle or large skillet to medium-high heat (375°F.). Grease lightly with oil. Griddle is ready when small drops of water sizzle and disappear almost immediately. Pancakes will stick if griddle is too cool.

2. In large bowl, beat eggs. Add buttermilk and oil; mix well. Add all remaining ingredients; stir just until large lumps disappear. For thicker pancakes, add additional flour; for thinner pancakes, add additional buttermilk.

3. For each pancake, pour about ¼ cup batter onto hot griddle. Cook 1 to 2 minutes or until bubbles begin to break on surface. Turn; cook 1 to 2 minutes or until golden brown.

Yield: 16 pancakes

TIP: * To substitute for buttermilk, use 2 tablespoons vinegar or lemon juice plus milk to make 2 cups.

APPLE PANCAKES: Add ½ cup shredded peeled apple and ½ teaspoon cinnamon to batter.

BLUEBERRY PANCAKES: Add 1 cup fresh or frozen blueberries to batter.

CHEESE PANCAKES: Add ½ cup shredded cheese to batter.

NUT PANCAKES: Add ½ cup chopped nuts to batter.

Whole Wheat Buttermilk Pancakes

Prep Time: 25 minutes

¾	cup Martha White® All Purpose Flour
¾	cup whole wheat flour
1½	teaspoons baking powder
¼	teaspoon baking soda
¼	teaspoon salt
2	tablespoons sugar
1	egg, beaten
1½	cups buttermilk*
3	tablespoons oil

1. Heat griddle or large skillet to medium heat (350°F.). Grease lightly with oil. Griddle is ready when small drops of water sizzle and disappear almost immediately. Pancakes will stick if griddle is too cool.

2. In large bowl, combine all ingredients; stir just until large lumps disappear. (Batter will be slightly lumpy.)

3. For each pancake, pour about ¼ cup batter onto hot griddle. Cook 1 to 1½ minutes or until bubbles begin to break on surface. Turn; cook 1 to 1½ minutes or until golden brown.

Yield: 14 pancakes

TIP: * To substitute for buttermilk, use 4½ teaspoons vinegar or lemon juice plus milk to make 1½ cups.

Muffin Mix Pancakes

Prep Time: 20 minutes

- 1 (7-oz.) pkg. Martha White® Apple Cinnamon, Blackberry, Blueberry, Cinnamon, Strawberry or Wildberry Muffin Mix
- ¾ cup milk
- 1 egg, slightly beaten

1. Heat griddle or large skillet to medium heat (350°F.). Grease lightly with oil. Griddle is ready when small drops of water sizzle and disappear almost immediately. Pancakes will stick if griddle is too cool.

2. In medium bowl, combine all ingredients; stir just until large lumps disappear. For thinner pancakes, add additional milk. (Batter will be slightly lumpy.)

3. For each pancake, pour about ¼ cup batter onto hot griddle. Cook 1 to 2 minutes or until bubbles begin to break on surface. Turn; cook 1 to 2 minutes or until golden brown.

Yield: 8 pancakes

Corn Meal Pancakes

Prep Time: 20 minutes

- 1½ cups Martha White® Self-Rising Corn Meal Mix
- ⅓ cup Martha White® Self-Rising Flour
- 1 teaspoon sugar
- 2 cups buttermilk*
- 2 tablespoons oil or melted shortening
- 1 egg, slightly beaten

1. Heat griddle or large skillet to medium heat (350°F.). Grease lightly with oil. Griddle is ready when small drops of water sizzle and disappear almost immediately. Pancakes will stick if griddle is too cool.

2. In large bowl, combine all ingredients; mix well.

3. For each pancake, pour about ¼ cup batter onto hot griddle. Cook 1 to 1½ minutes or until bubbles begin to break on surface. Turn; cook 1 to 1½ minutes or until golden brown.

Yield: 20 pancakes

TIP: * To substitute for buttermilk, use 2 tablespoons vinegar or lemon juice plus milk to make 2 cups.

Buttermilk and Sweet Milk

Sweet milk is simply fresh milk—not buttermilk. It's an old-fashioned Southern term commonly used to distinguish between the two in the days when folks churned their own butter and always had buttermilk on hand. Today's buttermilk is a cultured product usually made from low-fat milk. Buttermilk gives baked goods a moist texture and tangy flavor, while those made with sweet milk are milder in flavor.

Melt-in-your-Mouth Brunch Pancakes

Melt-in-your-Mouth Brunch Pancakes

A little sour cream does wonders for a basic pancake recipe. These pancakes have an almost ethereal texture worthy of the season's finest fresh fruits and whipped cream. No need for butter and syrup here.

Prep Time: 30 minutes

- 2 **cups Martha White® Self-Rising Flour**
- 1 **tablespoon sugar**
- ¼ **teaspoon baking soda**
- 2 **cups milk**
- ¼ **cup butter or margarine, melted**
- 1 **(8-oz.) container sour cream**
- 2 **eggs, beaten**
- 1 **cup whipping cream**
- 1 **tablespoon sugar**
- 5 **cups sweetened fresh or frozen raspberries, blueberries, strawberries, blackberries and/or sliced peeled peaches**

1. Heat griddle or large skillet to medium heat (350°F.). Grease lightly with oil. Griddle is ready when small drops of water sizzle and disappear almost immediately. Pancakes will stick if griddle is too cool.

2. In large bowl, combine flour, 1 tablespoon sugar and baking soda; mix well. In medium bowl, combine milk, butter, sour cream and eggs; blend well. Add to flour mixture; stir just until smooth. Batter should be very thin.

3. For each pancake, pour about ¼ cup batter onto hot griddle. Cook 1 to 1½ minutes or until bubbles begin to break on surface. Turn; cook 1 to 1½ minutes or until golden brown.

4. Meanwhile, in medium bowl, combine whipping cream and 1 tablespoon sugar; beat until stiff peaks form. To serve, spoon fruit on half of each pancake. Fold pancake over; top with additional fruit and whipped cream.

Yield: 20 pancakes

Tennessee Ernie Ford

Country superstar and Tennessee native, Tennessee Ernie Ford became the Martha White spokesperson in 1970 and remained so for almost two decades. America's favorite "Pea-Picker" performed in television and radio commercials, made guest appearances on the Grand Ole Opry, and performed private concerts for Martha White customers which helped expand distribution into new Southern markets. Ford gave one of his last performances in 1988 when Martha White Foods celebrated its 40th anniversary as a Grand Ole Opry sponsor. When Ford was introduced by country legend and friend Roy Acuff, the crowd rose to its feet.

Martha White spokesperson and America's favorite "Pea-Picker" Tennessee Ernie Ford.

Tennessee Ernie Ford was the first country performer to land a network television show and the first truly international country music celebrity. His recurring role on the "I Love Lucy" show is still seen by millions on cable television. "Sixteen Tons" is an enduring classic and Ford's powerful rendition of "Amazing Grace" made him a leading gospel music performer.

Country Waffles

Prep Time: 40 minutes

> 2   **eggs**
> 1¼   **cups milk**
> ½   **cup oil**
> 1¾   **cups Martha White® Self-Rising Flour**

1. Heat waffle iron. In large bowl, beat eggs. Add milk and oil; blend well. Add flour; mix well.

2. For each waffle, pour batter into hot waffle iron. Bake until steaming stops and waffle is golden brown.

Yield: 12 waffles

Corn Waffles

Prep Time: 40 minutes

> 1   **egg**
> 1½   **cups milk**
> 3   **tablespoons shortening, melted**
> 1   **cup Martha White® Self-Rising Corn Meal Mix**
> 1   **cup Martha White® Self-Rising Flour**
> 1   **tablespoon sugar**

1. Heat waffle iron. In large bowl, beat egg. Add milk and shortening; blend well. Add corn meal mix, flour and sugar; mix well.

2. For each waffle, pour batter into hot waffle iron. Bake until steaming stops and waffle is golden brown.

Yield: 12 waffles

Blueberry Almond Coffee Cake

Prep Time: 20 minutes
(Ready in 1 hour 15 minutes)

CAKE
> ½   **cup slivered blanched almonds**
> 1   **cup sour cream**
> ½   **cup milk**
> 2   **tablespoons sugar**
> 2   **(7-oz.) pkg. Martha White® Blueberry Muffin Mix**

GLAZE
> 1   **cup powdered sugar**
> 2   **tablespoons milk**
> ¼   **teaspoon almond extract**

1. Heat oven to 350°F. Grease 9-inch square pan. Spread almonds in single layer on ungreased cookie sheet. Bake at 350°F. for 5 to 7 minutes or until light golden brown. Cool 15 minutes. Chop almonds. Set aside.

2. In large bowl, combine sour cream, milk and sugar; mix well. Add muffin mix; stir to blend. Spread batter in greased pan. Sprinkle with almonds.

3. Bake at 350°F. for 35 to 40 minutes or until golden brown and cake begins to pull away from sides of pan.

4. Meanwhile, in small bowl, combine all glaze ingredients; blend until smooth.

5. Remove coffee cake from oven. Drizzle glaze over hot cake. Cool 10 to 15 minutes before serving.

Yield: 8 servings

Apple Upside-Down Skillet Coffee Cake

Use your well-seasoned iron skillet to make breakfast coffee cake. It cooks the apples just right and ensures that the cake will flip right out after it is baked.

Prep Time: 20 minutes (Ready in 50 minutes)

- ¼ cup butter or margarine
- 3 cups sliced peeled Golden Delicious apples
- ½ cup firmly packed brown sugar
- 1½ cups Martha White® Self-Rising Flour
- ½ cup sugar
- ½ cup butter or margarine, melted
- ½ cup milk
- 1 teaspoon vanilla
- 1 egg, beaten

1. Heat oven to 375°F. Melt ¼ cup butter in 10-inch cast iron skillet over medium heat. Stir in apples; cook about 5 minutes or just until tender, stirring occasionally. Stir in brown sugar. Set aside.

2. In medium bowl, combine flour and sugar; mix well. Stir in ½ cup melted butter, milk, vanilla and egg; blend until smooth. Pour batter over apples in skillet; spread batter evenly to edges.

3. Bake at 375°F. for 20 to 25 minutes or until golden brown. Remove from oven; cool 2 to 3 minutes. Invert coffee cake onto serving platter. Serve warm or cool.

Yield: 8 servings

Upside-Down Peach Coffee Cake

Prep Time: 15 minutes (Ready in 50 minutes)

TOPPING
- 2 tablespoons butter or margarine
- ¼ cup firmly packed brown sugar
- 1 cup peach or other flavor preserves
- ¼ cup chopped pecans
- 2 tablespoons grated orange peel

CAKE
- 1½ cups Martha White® Self-Rising Flour
- ¼ cup sugar
- ⅓ cup butter or margarine
- ½ cup milk
- 1 egg, slightly beaten

1. Heat oven to 400°F. Place 2 tablespoons butter in 9-inch round cake pan; heat in oven until butter is melted. Sprinkle brown sugar over melted butter.

2. In small bowl, combine preserves, pecans and orange peel; blend well. Spoon over brown sugar in pan; spread evenly.

3. In medium bowl, combine flour and sugar; mix well. Cut in ⅓ cup butter until mixture resembles coarse crumbs. In small bowl, combine milk and egg; blend well. Add to flour mixture; stir just until blended. Spread batter evenly over fruit mixture in pan.

4. Bake at 400°F. for 23 to 28 minutes or until top is golden brown. Cool 5 minutes; invert onto serving plate. Serve warm.

Yield: 8 servings

Orange Pecan Coffee Cake

Orange Pecan Coffee Cake

What a refreshing taste you'll get from adding orange to a coffee cake. Remember to grate the peel before squeezing the orange juice.

Prep Time: 20 minutes
(Ready in 1 hour 10 minutes)

CAKE
- 1 cup sugar
- 1 cup butter or margarine, softened
- 1 tablespoon grated orange peel
- 1 teaspoon vanilla
- 2 eggs
- 2 cups Martha White® Self-Rising Flour
- 1 cup sour cream

TOPPING
- ½ cup sugar
- 2 tablespoons Martha White® Self-Rising Flour
- ½ cup butter or margarine
- 1 cup chopped pecans

GLAZE
- 1 cup powdered sugar
- 4½ teaspoons orange juice

1. Heat oven to 350°F. Grease 13x9-inch pan. In large bowl, combine 1 cup sugar and 1 cup butter; beat until light and fluffy. Add orange peel, vanilla and eggs; blend well.

2. Add flour alternately with sour cream, beginning and ending with flour and mixing well after each addition. Spread batter in greased pan.

3. In medium bowl, combine ½ cup sugar and 2 tablespoons flour; mix well. With pastry blender or fork, cut in ½ cup butter until mixture resembles coarse crumbs. Stir in pecans. Sprinkle over batter in pan.

4. Bake at 350°F. for 35 to 40 minutes or until cake begins to pull away from sides of pan. Cool in pan on wire rack for 10 minutes.

5. Meanwhile, in small bowl, combine powdered sugar and orange juice; blend until smooth. Drizzle glaze over warm cake. Serve warm or cool.

Yield: 15 servings

Apple Streusel Coffee Cake

Prep Time: 20 minutes (Ready in 40 minutes)

CAKE
- 1 (7-oz.) pkg. Martha White® Apple Cinnamon Muffin Mix
- ½ cup milk
- 2 tablespoons butter or margarine, melted

TOPPING
- ⅓ cup firmly packed brown sugar
- ¼ cup chopped pecans
- 2 tablespoons Martha White® All Purpose Flour
- 2 tablespoons butter or margarine, softened

1. Heat oven to 350°F. Grease 8-inch square pan. In medium bowl, combine all cake ingredients; mix well. Pour into greased pan.

2. In small bowl, combine all topping ingredients; mix until crumbly. Sprinkle evenly over batter.

3. Bake at 350°F. for 18 to 20 minutes or until toothpick inserted in center comes out clean. Cool 5 to 10 minutes before serving.

Yield: 8 servings

Sour Cream Coffee Cake

Prep Time: 40 minutes
(Ready in 2 hours 40 minutes)

1½	cups sugar
1	cup butter or margarine, softened
3	eggs
1	teaspoon vanilla
3	cups Martha White® All Purpose Flour
2½	teaspoons baking powder
1	teaspoon salt
¼	teaspoon baking soda
1	cup sour cream
½	cup milk
½	cup chopped pecans
¼	cup firmly packed brown sugar
1	teaspoon cinnamon

1. Heat oven to 350°F. Grease and flour 12-cup Bundt® or 10-inch tube pan. In large bowl, combine sugar and butter; beat until light and fluffy. Add eggs 1 at a time, beating well after each addition. Add vanilla; blend well.

2. In large bowl, combine flour, baking powder, salt and baking soda; mix well. Add to butter mixture alternately with sour cream and milk, beginning and ending with flour mixture and mixing well after each addition. Spoon half of batter into greased and floured pan.

3. In small bowl, combine pecans, brown sugar and cinnamon; mix well. Sprinkle mixture evenly over batter in pan. Spoon remaining batter over filling.

4. Bake at 350°F. for 55 to 60 minutes or until toothpick inserted one inch from edge comes out clean. Cool in pan 10 minutes. Remove from pan. Cool 1 hour or until completely cooled.

Yield: 15 servings

SOUR CREAM POUND CAKE: Omit pecan, brown sugar and cinnamon layer.

Easy Fruit Coffee Cake

This easy basic batter takes on all kinds of seasonal tastes. Let whatever fruit is at its peak be your guide.

Prep Time: 20 minutes (Ready in 55 minutes)

CAKE

1½	cups Martha White® Self-Rising Flour
½	cup sugar
½	cup butter or margarine
½	cup milk
1	egg, beaten

TOPPING

3	cups sliced fresh plums, peaches, apples or pears
½	cup sugar
½	teaspoon cinnamon*
3	tablespoons butter or margarine, melted

1. Heat oven to 375°F. Grease 13x9-inch pan. In large bowl, combine flour and ½ cup sugar; mix well. With pastry blender or fork, cut in ½ cup butter until mixture resembles coarse crumbs. Add milk and egg; stir just until blended. Spread batter evenly in greased pan.

2. Arrange sliced fruit in rows over batter. In small bowl, combine ½ cup sugar and cinnamon; mix well. Sprinkle evenly over fruit. Drizzle with melted butter.

3. Bake at 375°F. for 28 to 35 minutes or until golden brown. Serve warm or cool.

Yield: 18 servings

TIP: * If using pears, omit cinnamon.

Easy Fruit Coffee Cake

Carolina Coffee Cake

This recipe has been a Martha White Kitchens favorite of Southern bakers for generations.

Prep Time: 20 minutes
(Ready in 1 hour 10 minutes)

CAKE
- ¾ cup sugar
- ⅓ cup shortening
- 2 eggs
- ¾ cup milk
- 1¾ cups Martha White® Self-Rising Flour
- ⅓ cup chopped pecans

CRUMB TOPPING
- ½ cup firmly packed brown sugar
- 2 tablespoons Martha White® Self-Rising Flour
- 1 teaspoon cinnamon
- 2 tablespoons butter or margarine, softened

ICING
- 1½ cups powdered sugar
- 2 tablespoons hot milk
- ½ teaspoon vanilla

1. Heat oven to 375°F. Grease 10-inch cast iron skillet or 9-inch square pan. In large bowl, combine sugar and shortening; beat until light and fluffy.

2. Add eggs 1 at a time, beating well after each addition. Add milk; beat until blended. Stir in 1¾ cups flour and pecans; blend well. Pour batter into greased skillet.

3. In small bowl, combine all crumb topping ingredients; mix until crumbly. Sprinkle over batter.

4. Bake at 375°F. for 30 to 35 minutes or until cake begins to pull away from sides of pan. Cool in pan 15 minutes.

5. In small bowl, combine all icing ingredients; stir until smooth. Drizzle over warm cake.

Yield: 15 servings

Muffin Mix Snack Cake

Prep Time: 15 minutes
(Ready in 1 hour 35 minutes)

CAKE
- 1 (7-oz.) pkg. Martha White® Low Fat Muffin Mix, any flavor
- ½ cup water

GLAZE
- ½ cup powdered sugar
- 1 tablespoon milk
- ¼ teaspoon vanilla

1. Heat oven to 350°F. Grease 8-inch square pan. In medium bowl, combine muffin mix and water; blend well. Pour into greased pan.

2. Bake at 350°F. for 15 to 20 minutes or until toothpick inserted in center comes out clean. Cool 1 hour or until completely cooled.

3. In small bowl, combine all glaze ingredients; blend until smooth. Drizzle glaze over cooled cake.

Yield: 8 servings

Blue Ridge Corn Meal Coffee Cake

A little self-rising corn meal mix gives this coffee cake a pleasing texture and just a hint of corn flavor.

**Prep Time: 20 minutes
(Ready in 1 hour 10 minutes)**

CAKE
1½ cups Martha White® Self-Rising Flour
½ cup Martha White® Self-Rising Corn Meal Mix
½ cup sugar
½ cup butter or margarine
½ cup milk
1 (8-oz.) container sour cream
¼ teaspoon almond extract
1 egg, beaten

TOPPING
2 cups fresh or frozen blueberries
⅓ cup sugar
2 tablespoons butter or margarine, melted
½ cup sliced almonds

1. Heat oven to 375°F. Grease 13x9-inch pan. In large bowl, combine flour, corn meal mix and ½ cup sugar; mix well. With pastry blender or fork, cut in ½ cup butter until mixture resembles coarse crumbs.

2. In small bowl, combine milk, sour cream, almond extract and egg; blend well. Add to flour mixture; stir just until blended. Spread batter evenly in greased pan.

3. Sprinkle blueberries over batter. Sprinkle with ⅓ cup sugar; drizzle with 2 tablespoons melted butter. Sprinkle with almonds.

4. Bake at 375°F. for 40 to 50 minutes or until edges are golden brown.

Yield: 15 servings

Easy Cream Cheese Danish

Prep Time: 20 minutes (Ready in 40 minutes)

CREAM CHEESE FILLING
2 (3-oz.) pkg. cream cheese, softened
3 tablespoons sugar
4 teaspoons Martha White® All Purpose Flour
1 egg

ROLLS
2 (5.5-oz.) pkg. Martha White® Bix Mix Buttermilk Biscuit Mix
3 to 4 tablespoons sugar
⅔ cup milk
⅓ cup butter or margarine, melted

GLAZE
1 cup powdered sugar
1 tablespoon warm water
¼ teaspoon vanilla

1. Heat oven to 450°F. Lightly grease 1 large or 2 medium cookie sheets. In small bowl, combine cream cheese and 3 tablespoons sugar; beat well. Add flour and egg; beat until smooth. Set aside.

2. In large bowl, combine biscuit mix and 3 to 4 tablespoons sugar; mix well. Add milk and melted butter; blend well. Drop dough by rounded tablespoonfuls onto greased cookie sheet, forming 16 mounds.

3. With back of spoon, make shallow indentation in center of each mound. Place heaping tablespoonful cream cheese filling into each indentation.

4. Bake at 450°F. for 12 to 15 minutes or until golden brown. Cool 5 minutes.

5. In small bowl, combine all glaze ingredients. Blend until smooth; drizzle over warm rolls.

Yield: 16 rolls

Main Dishes

Quick weekday suppers and more leisurely traditional Sunday dinners are both realities of the Southern table. When time allows, Southerners delight in a table laden with generous platters of fried chicken and baked ham surrounded by more side dishes than you can count and, of course, a basket of hot biscuits or cornbread. But times change, and food in the South continues to evolve. With a nod to the ingenuity of generations past, today's Southern cook is likely to fashion traditional ingredients into streamlined one-dish meals easy for any day of the week.

Chicken Stew with Classic Dumplings, page 83

Old-Fashioned Chicken and Dumplings

Here's a Southern recipe for authentic chicken and dumplings. Choose your favorite kind of dumpling—drop or rolled.

Prep Time: 1 hour (Ready in 2 hours)

CHICKEN
- 3 to 3½ lb. cut-up frying chicken
- 1 large onion, cut in half
- 1 large carrot, cut in half
- 1 large stalk celery, cut in half
- 2 quarts (8 cups) water
- 2 tablespoons butter or margarine
- 1 teaspoon salt
- ½ teaspoon pepper

DUMPLINGS
- 2 cups Martha White® Self-Rising Flour
- ⅓ cup shortening
- ½ cup chicken broth

1. In Dutch oven, combine chicken, onion, carrot, celery and water. Bring to a boil. Reduce heat to low; cover and simmer 1 hour or until tender.

2. Remove chicken from broth; cool chicken and broth slightly. Remove chicken from bones. Cut into bite-sized pieces; set aside. Skim fat from surface of cooled broth. Bring broth to a boil. Add butter, salt and pepper.

3. Place flour in bowl. With pastry blender or fork, cut in shortening until mixture resembles coarse crumbs. Add ½ cup chicken broth; stir with fork until dough leaves sides of bowl.

4. **For rolled dumplings:** On lightly floured surface, roll out dough to ⅛-inch thickness. Cut dough into strips or small squares.

5. **For drop dumplings:** On lightly floured surface, press out dough to ½-inch thickness. Pinch off dough in small pieces.

6. Drop dumplings 1 at a time into boiling broth. Reduce heat to low; cover and simmer 15 minutes or until dumplings are firm. Gently stir once or twice during cooking to prevent dumplings from sticking together. Stir chicken pieces into dumpling mixture just before serving.

Yield: 4 servings

Smoky White Bean Stew with Corn Meal Dumplings

Prep Time: 50 minutes

STEW
- 2 tablespoons oil
- 3 carrots, thinly sliced
- 1 large onion, chopped
- ½ lb. smoked sausage, cut into ½-inch slices
- 2 cups coarsely shredded cabbage
- 1 (15.5-oz.) can great northern beans, undrained
- 2 cups water
- 1 (14½-oz.) can ready-to-serve chicken broth
- ⅛ to ¼ teaspoon pepper
- 1 bay leaf

DUMPLINGS
- 1 cup Martha White® Self-Rising Flour
- ½ cup Martha White® Self-Rising Corn Meal Mix
- ¼ cup shortening
- 2 tablespoons chopped fresh parsley
- ½ teaspoon coarse ground black pepper
- ⅔ cup milk

1. Heat oil in 6-quart Dutch oven over medium-high heat until hot. Add carrots and onion; cook until tender, stirring occasionally. Add sausage; mix well. Cook until lightly browned, stirring occasionally.

2. Add all remaining stew ingredients. Bring to a boil. Reduce heat to low; simmer 15 to 20 minutes or until cabbage is tender. Remove and discard bay leaf.

3. In medium bowl, combine flour and corn meal mix. With pastry blender or fork, cut in shortening until mixture resembles coarse crumbs. Stir in parsley and pepper. Add milk; stir just until dry ingredients are moistened.

4. Drop dough by tablespoonfuls onto simmering stew. Cover; cook over medium-low heat for 10 to 15 minutes or until dumplings are firm.

Yield: 8 servings

Chicken Stew and Sausage Dumplings

Prep Time: 45 minutes

½	**lb. bulk pork sausage**
2	**tablespoons butter or margarine**
5	**stalks celery, cut into 1-inch pieces**
4	**carrots, cut into 1-inch pieces**
1	**large onion, chopped**
8½	**cups chicken broth**
½	**teaspoon pepper**
2	**cups Martha White® Self-Rising Flour**
¼	**cup shortening**
4	**cups cubed cooked chicken**

1. In medium skillet, cook sausage over medium heat until browned. Remove from skillet; drain on paper towels.

2. Meanwhile, melt butter in 8-quart Dutch oven over medium heat. Add celery, carrots and onion; cook until tender, stirring occasionally. Add 8 cups of the broth and the pepper. Bring to a boil. Reduce heat to low; simmer 15 minutes.

3. Place flour in large bowl. With pastry blender or fork, cut in shortening until mixture resembles coarse crumbs. Add cooked sausage and remaining ½ cup broth; stir with fork just until dough pulls away from sides of bowl.

4. Drop dough by heaping teaspoonfuls onto boiling stew. Reduce heat to low; cover and simmer 15 minutes or until dumplings are firm. Stir gently once or twice during cooking to prevent dumplings from sticking together. Carefully stir in chicken; cook until thoroughly heated.

Yield: 10 servings

Dumplings

If you're from the South, then a steaming bowl of chicken and dumplings is probably the first thing that comes to mind when you hear the words "soothing" and "comforting." Dumplings cooked with chicken or any kind of stew just seem to have mood-restoring properties that make you feel right with the world.

Besides just plain tasting good, dumplings were an economical way for cooks to extend a stew and make it more substantial. In fact, dumplings are a form of biscuits which are cooked in a pot instead of in the oven.

Like biscuits, there are two styles of dumplings—rolled and drop. For rolled dumplings, the dough is rolled out to about ⅛ inch thick, cut into strips or squares and gently lowered into a simmering broth. Even easier to prepare, drop dumplings are made with a softer biscuit dough that's simply dropped by spoonfuls into the pot.

Although they're best of friends, chicken is not the only accompaniment to dumplings. Try the streamlined Tomato Vegetable Stew with Cheddar Cheese Dumplings on page 83 or the Smoky White Bean Stew with Corn Meal Dumplings on page 80. The Sautéed Peaches with Butter Pecan Dumplings on page 212 are certainly worthy of fragrant summer peaches.

Tomato Vegetable Stew With Cheddar Cheese Dumplings

Tomato Vegetable Stew with Cheddar Cheese Dumplings

Prep Time: 50 minutes

STEW

- 2 tablespoons oil
- 2 large onions, coarsely chopped
- 2 stalks celery, coarsely chopped
- 2 cups frozen Italian green beans
- 1 (28-oz.) can diced tomatoes, undrained
- 1 (14½-oz.) can ready-to-serve chicken broth
- 1 teaspoon dried basil leaves
- ¼ teaspoon pepper

DUMPLINGS

- 1½ cups Martha White® Self-Rising Flour
- ½ teaspoon dry mustard
- ¼ cup shortening
- 2 oz. (½ cup) shredded sharp Cheddar cheese
- ⅔ cup milk

1. Heat oil in 6-quart Dutch oven or large saucepan over medium-high heat until hot. Add onions and celery; cook and stir until tender.

2. Add all remaining stew ingredients; mix well. Bring to a boil. Reduce heat to low; simmer 15 to 20 minutes or until beans are tender.

3. In medium bowl, combine flour and dry mustard; mix well. With pastry blender or fork, cut in shortening until mixture resembles coarse crumbs. Stir in cheese. Add milk; stir just until dry ingredients are moistened.

4. Drop dough by tablespoonfuls onto simmering stew. Cover; cook over medium-low heat for 10 to 15 minutes or until dumplings are firm.

Yield: 8 servings

Chicken Stew with Classic Dumplings

This streamlined chicken stew recipe takes advantage of canned broth and cooked chicken. The dumplings are dropped over the bubbling broth.

Prep Time: 45 minutes

STEW

- 2 tablespoons oil
- 4 stalks celery, coarsely chopped
- 3 carrots, thinly sliced
- 1 large onion, chopped
- 3 cups cubed cooked chicken
- ½ teaspoon pepper
- 6 cups chicken broth

DUMPLINGS

- 1½ cups Martha White® Self-Rising Flour
- ¼ cup shortening
- 2 tablespoons chopped fresh parsley
- ½ cup chicken broth

1. Heat oil in Dutch oven or large saucepan over medium-high heat until hot. Add celery, carrots and onion; cook and stir until tender. Add chicken, pepper and 6 cups broth. Bring to a boil. Reduce heat to medium-low; simmer 15 minutes.

2. Place flour in medium bowl. With pastry blender or fork, cut in shortening until mixture resembles coarse crumbs. Stir in parsley. Add ½ cup broth; stir just until dry ingredients are moistened.

3. Drop dough by tablespoonfuls onto simmering stew. Cover; cook over medium-low heat for 10 to 15 minutes or until dumplings are firm.

Yield: 8 servings

Smothered Chicken Bake with Black Pepper Biscuits

Prep Time: 30 minutes (Ready in 1 hour)

FILLING

- 2 tablespoons butter or margarine
- 3 carrots, sliced
- 3 stalks celery, sliced
- 1 large onion, cut into thin wedges
- 1 (10¾-oz.) can condensed cream of celery soup
- ¾ cup chicken broth
- 3 cups cubed cooked chicken

BISCUITS

- 1½ cups Martha White® Self-Rising Flour
- ½ cup butter or margarine, melted
- ⅓ cup milk
- ¾ teaspoon coarse ground black pepper

1. Heat oven to 400°F. Grease shallow 2-quart casserole. Melt butter in large skillet over medium-high heat. Add carrots, celery and onion; cook 7 to 8 minutes or until crisp-tender, stirring occasionally. Add soup and broth; mix well.

2. Spread chicken in greased casserole. Spoon vegetable mixture over chicken.

3. In medium bowl, combine all biscuit ingredients; stir with fork just until dry ingredients are moistened. Drop dough by tablespoonfuls over chicken mixture.

4. Bake at 400°F. for 25 to 30 minutes or until biscuits are golden brown.

Yield: 6 servings

Italian Breakfast Cobbler

An easy self-rising-flour batter enriched with lots of eggs becomes crisp on top and forms a quiche-like layer around a filling of Italian sausage and spinach.

Prep Time: 20 minutes (Ready in 1 hour)

FILLING

- 1 lb. bulk Italian sausage
- 1 tablespoon oil
- 1 large onion, coarsely chopped
- 1 large red bell pepper, coarsely chopped
- 1 (8-oz.) pkg. fresh whole mushrooms, sliced
- 2 (9-oz.) pkg. frozen spinach in a pouch, thawed, drained
- 8 oz. (2 cups) shredded mozzarella or provolone cheese

TOPPING

- 1½ cups Martha White® Self-Rising Flour
- ½ cup grated Parmesan cheese
- 1¼ cups milk
- ½ cup butter or margarine, melted
- 5 eggs, beaten

1. Heat oven to 400°F. Grease 13x9-inch (3-quart) baking dish. In large skillet, cook sausage over medium-high heat for 8 minutes or until browned. Remove from skillet; drain.

2. Heat oil in same skillet over medium-high heat until hot. Add onion and bell pepper; cook 5 minutes. Add mushrooms; cook 3 minutes or until vegetables are tender.

3. Stir in spinach and cooked sausage. Pour into greased baking dish. Sprinkle with cheese.

4. In medium bowl, combine all topping ingredients. With wire whisk, beat until smooth. Pour over filling in baking dish.

5. Bake at 400°F. for 35 to 40 minutes or until golden brown.

Yield: 10 servings

Italian Breakfast Cobbler

Fiesta Breakfast Cobbler

Prep Time: 30 minutes
(Ready in 1 hour 30 minutes)

FILLING

1	tablespoon oil
1	large onion, coarsely chopped
1	large bell pepper, coarsely chopped
2	(15.5-oz.) cans pinto beans, drained
1	(10-oz.) can diced tomatoes and green chiles, undrained
1	(9-oz.) pkg. frozen corn in a pouch, thawed
12	oz. pasteurized processed cheese spread, cubed (3 cups)

TOPPING

1	cup Martha White® Self-Rising Flour
½	cup Martha White® Self-Rising Corn Meal Mix
1	teaspoon chili powder
¼	teaspoon cumin
1¼	cups milk
½	cup butter or margarine, melted
4	eggs, beaten

1. Heat oven to 400°F. Grease 13x9-inch (3-quart) baking dish. Heat oil in large skillet over medium-high heat until hot. Add onion and bell pepper; cook until tender, stirring occasionally.

2. Remove skillet from heat. Add beans, tomatoes, corn and cheese spread; mix well. Pour into greased baking dish.

3. In medium bowl, combine all topping ingredients; stir until smooth. Pour batter over filling in baking dish.

4. Bake at 400°F. for 40 to 45 minutes or until golden brown.

Yield: 10 servings

Country Breakfast Cobbler

Prep Time: 30 minutes
(Ready in 1 hour 10 minutes)

FILLING

1	tablespoon oil
1	large onion, chopped
4	cups frozen hash-brown potatoes
3	cups chopped cooked ham*
⅓	cup chopped fresh parsley
6	oz. (1½ cups) shredded Cheddar cheese

TOPPING

1½	cups Martha White® Self-Rising Flour
½	teaspoon coarse ground black pepper
1¼	cups milk
½	cup butter or margarine, melted
5	eggs, beaten

1. Heat oven to 400°F. Grease 13x9-inch (3-quart) baking dish. Heat oil in large skillet over medium-high heat until hot. Add onion; cook until tender, stirring occasionally. Add potatoes and ham; mix well. Remove from heat. Stir in parsley. Pour into greased baking dish. Sprinkle with cheese.

2. In medium bowl, combine all topping ingredients; beat with wire whisk until smooth. Pour batter over filling in baking dish.

3. Bake at 400°F. for 35 to 40 minutes or until golden brown.

Yield: 10 servings

TIP: * One lb. bulk pork sausage, cooked and drained, can be substituted for the ham.

Next Day Turkey Pot Pie

Prep Time: 35 minutes
(Ready in 1 hour 25 minutes)

FILLING
1   tablespoon oil
1   medium onion, chopped
1   cup thinly sliced carrots
1   cup thinly sliced celery
1   (9-oz.) pkg. frozen spinach in a pouch, thawed, drained
3   cups cubed cooked turkey
½   cup chopped country or baked ham
1   (10¾-oz.) can condensed cream of chicken soup
1   cup milk
¼   teaspoon pepper

TOPPING
1½   cups Martha White® Self-Rising Flour
¼   cup grated Parmesan cheese
1½   cups milk
½   cup butter or margarine, melted

1. Heat oven to 400°F. Grease 13x9-inch (3-quart) baking dish. Heat oil in large skillet over medium heat until hot. Add onion, carrots and celery; cook and stir until tender, stirring occasionally.

2. Stir in spinach. Spread mixture evenly in greased baking dish. Sprinkle turkey and ham evenly over spinach mixture.

3. In medium bowl, combine soup, 1 cup milk and pepper; mix well. Pour soup mixture evenly over turkey and ham. In same medium bowl, combine all topping ingredients; stir until smooth. Pour over soup mixture.

4. Bake at 400°F. for 40 to 50 minutes or until golden brown.

Yield: 8 servings

TIP: For individual servings, grease six 2-cup baking dishes. Spoon filling evenly into dishes. Top each with topping batter. Bake as directed above.

Country Italian Sausage Pie

Instead of classic polenta, a crown of cheesy cornbread tops a savory filling.

Prep Time: 30 minutes (Ready in 1 hour)

1   lb. mild or hot Italian sausage links
1   tablespoon oil
2   large green or red bell peppers, cut into thin strips
1   large onion, cut into thin wedges
1   (14.5-oz.) can diced tomatoes, undrained
1   (6-oz.) pkg. Martha White® Cotton Pickin' or Buttermilk Cornbread Mix
½   cup milk
1   egg, beaten
4   oz. (1 cup) shredded mozzarella cheese

1. Heat oven to 400°F. Grease 13x9-inch (3-quart) baking dish. Cut each sausage link into 4 pieces. Heat oil in large skillet over medium-high heat until hot. Add sausage; cook and stir until browned.

2. Add bell peppers and onion; cook until vegetables are tender, stirring occasionally. Stir in tomatoes; cook 2 to 3 minutes. Pour into greased baking dish.

3. In small bowl, combine cornbread mix, milk and egg; stir until smooth. Stir in cheese. Spoon batter around edge of mixture in baking dish.

4. Bake at 400°F. for 25 to 30 minutes or until topping is golden brown.

Yield: 8 servings

Chicken à la King Pot Pie

Prep Time: 30 minutes
(Ready in 1 hour 15 minutes)

FILLING
2 tablespoons butter or margarine
2 cups sliced fresh mushrooms
1 medium onion, chopped
1 (10¾-oz.) can condensed cream of
   mushroom soup
1 (2-oz.) jar chopped pimientos, drained
½ cup milk
1 teaspoon Worcestershire sauce
3 cups cubed cooked chicken

TOPPING
1 cup Martha White® Self-Rising Flour
1 cup milk
½ cup butter or margarine, melted
2 tablespoons chopped fresh parsley

1. Heat oven to 400°F. Grease shallow 2-quart casserole. Melt 2 tablespoons butter in large skillet over medium-high heat. Add mushrooms and onion; cook until tender, stirring occasionally. Stir in soup, pimientos, ½ cup milk and Worcestershire sauce.

2. Spread chicken in greased casserole. Pour mushroom mixture over chicken. In medium bowl, combine all topping ingredients; stir until smooth. Pour over chicken mixture in casserole.

3. Bake at 400°F. for 40 to 45 minutes or until golden brown.

Yield: 6 servings

Savory Sausage Chicken Pie

Prep Time: 30 minutes
(Ready in 1 hour)

1 lb. bulk pork sausage
1 cup thinly sliced carrots
1 cup thinly sliced celery
½ cup chopped onion
2 cups cubed cooked chicken
1 (10¾-oz.) can condensed cream of
   celery soup
½ cup milk
2 cups Martha White® Self-Rising Flour
¼ cup butter or margarine
⅔ cup milk

1. Heat oven to 400°F. Grease 2-quart casserole. In large skillet, combine sausage, carrots, celery and onion; cook over medium heat until sausage is browned and vegetables are tender, stirring occasionally. Drain. Stir in chicken, soup and ½ cup milk.

2. Place flour in large bowl. With pastry blender or fork, cut in butter until mixture resembles coarse crumbs. Add ⅔ cup milk; stir until dough leaves sides of bowl. Press half of dough into bottom of greased casserole. Pour sausage mixture over dough. Drop remaining dough by tablespoonfuls over sausage mixture.

3. Bake at 400°F. for 25 to 30 minutes or until sausage mixture is hot and bubbly and biscuits are golden brown.

Yield: 8 servings

Savory Sausage Chicken Pie

Chicken Country Captain Pie

This recipe was inspired by Country Captain, a traditional curried chicken stew from the Georgia coast.

**Prep Time: 30 minutes
(Ready in 1 hour 5 minutes)**

FILLING
- 3 **slices bacon, chopped**
- 1 **medium onion, chopped**
- 1 **medium green bell pepper, cut into thin slices**
- 1 **garlic clove, minced**
- 1 **tablespoon curry powder**
- 2 **(14.5-oz.) cans diced tomatoes, undrained**
- 3 **cups cubed cooked chicken**
- ⅓ **cup golden raisins**
- ½ **teaspoon salt**

CRUST
- 1 **cup Martha White® Self-Rising Flour**
- 1 **tablespoon sugar**
- ⅓ **cup butter or margarine**
- ⅓ **cup slivered almonds, toasted***
- 6 **tablespoons cold water**

1. Heat oven to 400°F. Grease shallow 2-quart casserole. In large skillet, cook bacon over medium heat until crisp. Drain on paper towels. Reserve drippings.

2. Add onion, bell pepper, garlic and curry powder to drippings in skillet; cook until vegetables are tender, stirring occasionally. Stir in tomatoes, chicken, raisins, salt and cooked bacon. Bring to a boil. Spoon into greased casserole.

3. In medium bowl, combine flour and sugar. With pastry blender or fork, cut in butter until mixture resembles coarse crumbs. Add almonds; mix well. Add water; stir with fork until soft dough forms and mixture begins to pull away from sides of bowl.

4. On lightly floured surface, knead dough gently 5 times or just until smooth. Pat into shape to fit in greased casserole. Gently place dough over chicken mixture.

5. Bake at 400°F. for 30 to 35 minutes or until golden brown.

Yield: 6 servings

TIP: * To toast almonds, spread on cookie sheet. Bake at 350°F. for 5 to 7 minutes or until golden brown, stirring occasionally.

Kielbasa Bean Bake

**Prep Time: 30 minutes
(Ready in 1 hour 15 minutes)**

- 1 **lb. smoked kielbasa, sliced**
- 1 **cup thin onion wedges**
- 2 **(16-oz.) cans pork and beans**
- 1 **(6-oz.) pkg. Martha White® Buttermilk Cornbread Mix**
- ⅔ **cup milk**
- 1 **(11-oz.) can vacuum-packed whole kernel corn, drained**

1. Heat oven to 400°F. Grease shallow 4-quart casserole or 13x9-inch (3-quart) baking dish. In large skillet, cook sausage and onion over medium-high heat until sausage is browned and onions are tender. Stir in beans. Pour into greased baking dish.

2. In medium bowl, combine cornbread mix and milk; stir until smooth. Stir in corn. Pour batter over sausage mixture in casserole.

3. Bake at 400°F. for 40 to 45 minutes or until golden brown.

Yield: 6 servings

Chicken Country Captain Pie

Easy Pickin' Chicken Pie

This comforting combination of creamy chicken and vegetables topped with a buttery crust is a Martha White Kitchens classic.

Prep Time: 20 minutes
(Ready in 1 hour 10 minutes)

3	cups cubed cooked chicken
1⅓	cups frozen mixed vegetables, thawed
1	(10¾-oz.) can condensed cream of celery soup
1	cup chicken broth
¼	teaspoon pepper
1	cup Martha White® Self-Rising Flour
1	cup milk
½	cup butter or margarine, melted

1. Heat oven to 400°F. Grease shallow 2-quart casserole. Spread chicken and vegetables evenly in bottom of greased dish.

2. In medium bowl, combine soup, broth and pepper; mix well. Pour evenly over chicken mixture.

3. In another medium bowl, combine flour, milk and butter; stir until smooth. Pour over chicken mixture in casserole.

4. Bake at 400°F. for 45 to 50 minutes or until golden brown. Let stand 10 minutes before serving.

Yield: 6 servings

Chicken Enchilada Cornbread Pie

Prep Time: 20 minutes
(Ready in 55 minutes)

2	cups cubed cooked chicken
8	oz. pasteurized process cheese spread, cubed (2 cups)
1	(15.5-oz.) can pinto beans, drained
1	(2¼-oz.) can sliced ripe olives, drained
½	cup salsa
2	tablespoons chili powder
¼	teaspoon garlic powder
1	cup Martha White® Self-Rising Corn Meal Mix
½	cup milk
3	tablespoons oil
1	egg, beaten
	Toppings, such as chopped tomatoes, shredded lettuce, chopped green onions, avocado slices, salsa and/or sour cream, if desired

1. Heat oven to 400°F. Grease 8-inch square (2-quart) baking dish. In large bowl, combine chicken, cheese spread, beans, olives, salsa, chili powder and garlic powder; mix well. Pour into greased baking dish.

2. In small bowl, combine corn meal mix, milk, oil and egg; stir until smooth. Pour over chicken mixture in baking dish.

3. Bake at 400°F. for 30 to 35 minutes or until golden brown. Serve with desired toppings.

Yield: 8 servings

Chicken Enchilada Cornbread Pie

Chili Dog Pie

This kid-pleasing recipe was created by Karen Shankles of Knoxville, Tennessee, for the 1997 National Cornbread Cook-Off.

Prep Time: 25 minutes (Ready in 50 minutes)

CHILI
- 1 **lb. ground beef**
- ½ **lb. hot dogs, cut into ½-inch pieces**
- 1 **cup salsa**
- 1 **(6-oz.) can tomato paste**
- 2 **teaspoons chili powder**
- ½ **teaspoon cumin**
  Salt and pepper

TOPPING
- 1 **(6-oz.) pkg. Martha White® Cotton Pickin' or Buttermilk Cornbread Mix**
- 4 **oz. (1 cup) shredded Cheddar cheese**
- 1 **(4.5-oz.) can chopped green chiles, undrained**
- ½ **cup milk**
- 1 **egg, beaten**

GARNISH
- ½ **cup chopped green onions**
- 4 **oz. (1 cup) shredded Cheddar cheese**

1. Heat oven to 450°F. In 10-inch cast iron or ovenproof skillet, brown ground beef over medium heat until thoroughly cooked. Drain. Stir in all remaining chili ingredients. Add salt and pepper to taste. Bring to a boil. Reduce heat to low; simmer 10 to 15 minutes or until mixture is thick.

2. In large bowl, combine all topping ingredients; blend well. Spoon batter around edge of chili in skillet.

3. Bake at 450°F. for 20 to 25 minutes or until topping is golden brown. Serve with green onions and additional Cheddar cheese.

Yield: 6 servings

Alabama Country Supper

This winning combination of apples and sausage baked under cornbread brought honors to Rosemary Johnson of Irondale, Alabama, at the 1998 National Cornbread Cook-Off.

Prep Time: 30 minutes (Ready in 50 minutes)

FILLING
- 1½ **lb. pork sausage patties**
- 6 **cups sliced peeled Golden Delicious or Granny Smith apples**
- ½ **cup dried cherries**
- 1 **cup sugar**
- ¼ **cup butter or margarine**

TOPPING
- 1 **(6-oz.) pkg. Martha White® Buttermilk or Cotton Pickin' Cornbread Mix**
- ½ **cup milk**
- 2 **tablespoons butter or margarine, melted**
- 1 **egg, beaten**

1. Heat oven to 425°F. In 10-inch cast iron or ovenproof skillet, cook sausage patties over medium heat until thoroughly cooked, turning once. Remove from skillet. Drain on paper towels; discard drippings.

2. In same skillet, combine apples, cherries, sugar and ¼ cup butter; cook over medium heat until apples are tender, stirring occasionally. Add cooked sausage to mixture in skillet, tucking patties under apples.

3. In medium bowl, combine all topping ingredients; stir until smooth. Pour evenly over sausage mixture.

4. Bake at 425°F. for 15 to 20 minutes or until golden brown.

Yield: 8 servings

Barbecue and Cornbread Bake

What could be easier? A cornbread mix baked over ground beef and flavored with bottled barbecue sauce.

Prep Time: 15 minutes (Ready in 40 minutes)

FILLING

1	lb. ground beef
1	medium onion, chopped
⅓	cup barbecue sauce
1	(8-oz.) can tomato sauce

TOPPING

1	(6-oz.) pkg. Martha White® Buttermilk Cornbread Mix
½	cup frozen whole kernel corn
½	cup milk
1	egg, beaten

1. Heat oven to 425°F. Grease 12x8-inch (2-quart) baking dish. In large skillet, cook ground beef and onion over medium-high heat for 8 to 10 minutes or until beef is thoroughly cooked, stirring occasionally. Drain. Add barbecue sauce and tomato sauce; mix well. Pour into greased baking dish.

2. In medium bowl, combine all topping ingredients; blend well. Spoon over beef mixture in baking dish; spread evenly.

3. Bake at 425°F. for 17 to 23 minutes or until golden brown.

Yield: 6 servings

Is It Dinner or Supper? What about Lunch?

In the Old South, dinner was served at noontime. And we're not talking a sandwich and chips—that's lunch. Dinner was the big meal of the day, served when farmers could escape the hot midday sun. Town folks, working just minutes away, could easily return to the home table graced with generous helpings of meat, vegetables and cornbread or biscuits. The evening meal, historically a lighter meal featuring dinner leftovers, was called supper.

It's Chicken for Supper

According to the National Broiler Council, each of us eats more than 70 lbs. of chicken annually, and the amount keeps increasing. That's more than the per capita consumption of any other meat—beef, pork, turkey or seafood. Of course, this doesn't surprise anyone in the South, where folks have long had a special fondness for chicken. Some would argue that fried chicken is the South's culinary gift to the world. Or, maybe it's chicken and dumplings. Those aren't the only chicken classics claimed by the South. Chicken Country Captain Pie on page 90 was inspired by the spicy-sweet tomato chicken curry dish brought to the Georgia coast by sea captains sailing from India. No one knows why Chicken à la King became a specialty of Southern hostesses back in the 1930s and 1940s. The updated Martha White version is on page 88. And you can't get any more Southern than Smothered Chicken Bake with Black Pepper Biscuits, on page 84.

Barbecued Beef and Cornbread Casserole

Prep Time: 15 minutes (Ready in 55 minutes)

- 1½ lb. ground beef
- ¼ cup chopped onion
- 1½ cups barbecue sauce
- 1 (16-oz.) can baked beans
- 2 cups Martha White® Self-Rising Corn Meal Mix
- 1½ cups buttermilk*
- ¼ cup oil
- 4 oz. (1 cup) shredded Cheddar cheese

1. Heat oven to 400°F. In large skillet, brown ground beef with onion over medium-high heat until beef is thoroughly cooked. Drain. Add barbecue sauce and beans; mix well. Cook until bubbly, stirring occasionally. Pour into ungreased 2½-quart casserole.

2. In medium bowl, combine corn meal mix, buttermilk and oil; stir until smooth. Spoon over beef mixture in casserole; spread evenly.

3. Bake at 400°F. for 35 to 40 minutes or until light golden brown. Sprinkle with cheese; bake an additional 3 minutes or until cheese is melted.

Yield: 8 servings

TIP: * To substitute for buttermilk, use 4½ teaspoons vinegar or lemon juice plus milk to make 1½ cups.

Beans and Cornbread Casserole

Tradition can be surprisingly convenient. Just combine spicy canned beans and cornbread mix for a nutritious, satisfying and quick supper.

Prep Time: 40 minutes

- 2 (15-oz.) cans spicy chili beans, drained
- 1 (14.5-oz.) can Mexican-style diced tomatoes, undrained
- 1 (6-oz.) pkg. Martha White® Buttermilk Cornbread Mix
- ⅔ cup milk
- 1 egg, beaten
- 4 oz. (1 cup) shredded Cheddar cheese Toppings, such as chopped tomatoes, shredded lettuce, chopped green onions, sliced ripe olives, salsa and/or sour cream, if desired

1. Heat oven to 400°F. In 10-inch cast iron or ovenproof skillet, combine chili beans and tomatoes. Bring to a boil over medium heat, stirring occasionally.

2. In small bowl, combine cornbread mix, milk and egg; stir until smooth. Pour over bean mixture in skillet.

3. Bake at 400°F. for 15 minutes or until light golden brown. Sprinkle with cheese; bake an additional 5 minutes or until cheese is melted. Let stand 10 minutes before serving. Serve with desired toppings.

Yield: 6 servings

Beans and Cornbread Casserole

Canyon Casserole

Prep Time: 25 minutes (Ready in 1 hour)

- 1 lb. ground beef
- 1 (14.5-oz.) can diced tomatoes, undrained
- 1 (7-oz.) can vacuum-packed whole kernel corn, drained
- ½ cup water
- 1 (1¼-oz.) pkg. taco seasoning mix
- 1 cup Martha White® Self-Rising Corn Meal Mix
- ½ cup milk
- 2 tablespoons oil
- 1 egg, beaten
- 4 oz. (1 cup) shredded Cheddar cheese

1. Heat oven to 400°F. Grease 8-inch square (2-quart) baking dish or shallow 2-quart casserole. In large skillet, brown ground beef over medium-high heat until thoroughly cooked. Drain.

2. Add tomatoes, corn, water and taco seasoning mix. Bring to a boil, stirring occasionally. Pour into greased baking dish.

3. In small bowl, combine corn meal mix, milk, oil and egg; blend well. Stir in cheese. Pour batter over ground beef mixture in baking dish.

4. Bake at 400°F. for 30 to 35 minutes or until golden brown.

Yield: 6 servings

Beans and Greens under Cornbread

This Martha White Kitchens favorite brings together the best of Southern cooking—crispy cornbread, greens, white beans and country ham.

Prep Time: 20 minutes (Ready in 50 minutes)

FILLING
- 1 tablespoon oil
- 1 large onion, cut into thin wedges
- 2 (15.5-oz.) cans great northern beans, drained, rinsed
- 1 (14.5-oz.) can diced tomatoes, undrained
- 1 (10-oz.) pkg. frozen chopped turnip greens, kale or collards, thawed, drained
- ½ cup chopped cooked country or sugar-cured ham

TOPPING
- 1 cup Martha White® Self-Rising Corn Meal Mix
- ½ cup milk
- ¼ cup oil
- 1 egg, beaten

1. Heat oven to 425°F. Heat oil in large cast iron or ovenproof skillet over medium-high heat until hot. Add onion; cook 3 to 5 minutes or until onion is crisp-tender, stirring occasionally.

2. Add all remaining filling ingredients; mix well. Cook 2 to 3 minutes or until thoroughly heated, stirring occasionally.

3. In medium bowl, combine all topping ingredients; stir until smooth. Spoon batter around edge of hot mixture in baking dish.

4. Bake at 425°F. for 25 to 30 minutes or until topping is golden brown.

Yield: 6 servings

Beans and Greens under Cornbread

Chicken and Cornbread Dressing Casserole

This Sunday dinner classic has been streamlined for the weeknight rush. Sage-seasoned cornbread is baked over a creamy chicken filling.

Prep Time: 15 minutes (Ready in 50 minutes)

FILLING

2	cups diced cooked chicken
1⅓	cups frozen mixed vegetables, thawed
1	(10¾-oz.) can condensed cream of chicken soup
½	cup milk
¼	teaspoon pepper

CRUST

¼	cup butter or margarine
1	cup chopped onions
½	cup chopped celery
1	cup Martha White® Self-Rising Corn Meal Mix
½	teaspoon dried sage leaves
½	cup milk
1	egg, beaten

1. Heat oven to 400°F. Grease 10x6-inch (1½-quart) baking dish. Spread chicken and mixed vegetables in greased baking dish. In medium bowl, combine soup, ½ cup milk and pepper; blend well. Pour over chicken mixture.

2. Melt butter in large skillet over medium heat. Add onions and celery; cook 5 to 7 minutes or until vegetables are tender.

3. In medium bowl, combine corn meal mix, sage, ½ cup milk, egg and cooked onion mixture; blend well. Pour around edges of mixture in baking dish.

4. Bake at 425°F. for 30 to 35 minutes or until golden brown.

Yield: 6 servings

Delta Supper

Prep Time: 30 minutes (Ready in 1 hour)

3	tablespoons oil
1	lb. smoked sausage, cut into 1-inch pieces
2	large green bell peppers, cut into strips
1	large onion, cut into thin wedges
2	(15-oz.) cans black-eyed peas, drained
1	(14.5-oz.) can diced tomatoes, undrained
1	cup Martha White® Self-Rising Corn Meal Mix
¼	teaspoon ground red pepper (cayenne)
⅔	cup milk
1	egg, beaten

1. Heat oven to 400°F. Grease 13x9-inch (3-quart) baking dish. Heat 1 tablespoon of the oil in large skillet over medium-high heat until hot. Add sausage, bell peppers and onion; cook until sausage is browned and vegetables are tender, stirring occasionally.

2. Add black-eyed peas and tomatoes; mix well. Reduce heat to low; simmer 5 minutes. Pour into greased baking dish.

3. In small bowl, combine corn meal mix, ground red pepper, milk and egg; stir until smooth. Pour over sausage mixture in baking dish.

4. Bake at 400°F. for 25 to 30 minutes or until golden brown.

Yield: 8 servings

Delta Supper

Country-Style Chili con Cornbread

**Prep Time: 30 minutes
(Ready in 2 hours 35 minutes)**

CHILI

1	lb. bulk pork sausage
1	lb. ground beef
1	medium onion, chopped
1	medium green bell pepper, chopped
1	garlic clove, minced
2	(15.5-oz.) cans red kidney beans, drained
1	(28-oz.) can peeled whole tomatoes, undrained
1	cup water
3	teaspoons chili powder
2	teaspoons cumin
½	teaspoon salt
½	teaspoon ground red pepper (cayenne)

TOPPING

1½	cups Martha White® Self-Rising Corn Meal Mix
¾	cup milk
¼	cup oil
1	egg, beaten
6	oz. (1½ cups) shredded sharp Cheddar cheese

1. In large saucepan, cook sausage, ground beef, onion, bell pepper and garlic over medium-high heat until sausage and ground beef are thoroughly cooked and vegetables are tender, stirring occasionally. Drain.

2. Stir in all remaining chili ingredients. Crush tomatoes with back of wooden spoon. Reduce heat to low; cover and simmer 1 to 1½ hours. Additional water may be added if necessary.

3. Heat oven to 400°F. Spoon chili into ungreased 13x9-inch (3-quart) baking dish. In medium bowl, combine corn meal mix, milk, oil, egg and 1 cup of the cheese; blend well. Spoon batter over chili in baking dish. Sprinkle with remaining ½ cup cheese.

4. Bake at 400°F. for 30 to 35 minutes or until golden brown.

Yield: 8 servings

Good Luck Black-Eyed Pea and Sausage Bake

Ensure good luck for the New Year, and good eating all year long, with this all-in-one dish featuring black-eyed peas under a crispy blanket of cornbread.

Prep Time: 30 minutes (Ready in 1 hour)

FILLING

1	lb. smoke-flavored bulk pork sausage
1	large onion, cut into thin wedges
1	large bell pepper, cut into short thin strips
2	garlic cloves, minced
2	(15-oz.) cans black-eyed peas, drained
1	(14.5-oz.) can diced tomatoes, undrained
½	teaspoon dried thyme leaves
1	(10-oz.) pkg. frozen okra, thawed, if desired

TOPPING

1½	cups Martha White® Self-Rising Corn Meal Mix
1	teaspoon coarse ground black pepper
1	cup buttermilk*
¼	cup oil
1	egg, beaten

1. Heat oven to 425°F. Grease 13x9-inch (3-quart) baking dish. In large skillet, cook sausage over medium-high heat for 7 to 8 minutes or until browned. Add onion, bell pepper and garlic; cook until vegetables are tender, stirring occasionally.

2. Stir in black-eyed peas, tomatoes and thyme; cook 2 to 3 minutes or until thoroughly heated. Stir in okra. Pour into greased baking dish.

3. In medium bowl, combine all topping ingredients; stir until smooth. Spoon batter around edge of sausage mixture in baking dish.

4. Bake at 425°F. for 25 to 30 minutes or until topping is golden brown.

Yield: 10 servings

TIP: * To substitute for buttermilk, use 1 tablespoon vinegar or lemon juice plus milk to make 1 cup.

Cajun Cornbread Skillet

Prep Time: 25 minutes (Ready in 1 hour)

- ¼ cup oil
- 1 lb. andouille or smoked sausage, sliced
- 1 large onion, chopped
- 1 large green bell pepper, chopped
- 1 cup Martha White® Self-Rising Corn Meal Mix
- ¾ cup buttermilk*
- 2 eggs, beaten
- 1 (8.5-oz.) can cream-style corn
- 4 oz. (1 cup) shredded Cheddar cheese

1. Heat oven to 400°F. Heat 1 tablespoon of the oil in 10-inch cast iron or ovenproof skillet over medium-high heat until hot. Add sausage, onion and bell pepper; cook until sausage is browned and vegetables are tender, stirring occasionally.

2. In large bowl, combine corn meal mix, buttermilk, eggs and remaining 3 tablespoons oil; blend well. Add corn, cheese and cooked sausage mixture. Wipe skillet clean with paper towel; spray with nonstick cooking spray. Pour batter into skillet.

3. Bake at 400°F. for 25 to 35 minutes or until golden brown and set.

Yield: 10 servings

TIP: * To substitute for buttermilk, use 2¼ teaspoons vinegar or lemon juice plus milk to make ¾ cup.

Guarantee a Little Good Luck

The old saying goes that a New Year's Day menu of black-eyed peas for luck and a pot of greens for riches is the surest way to happiness all year long. Traditionalists simmer a pot of dried black-eyed peas with their leftover holiday ham bone and boil a pot of turnip, mustard, kale or collard greens for hours. The not-so-traditional may opt to bring in the New Year with new-style Border Corn Cakes with Black-Eyed Pea Salsa, page 218, or all-in-one Good-Luck Black-Eyed Pea and Sausage Bake, page 102.

Festive Good Luck Cornbread Skillet

Karen Shackles of Knoxville, Tennessee, can take a bow for this recipe, which won the grand prize in the 1998 National Cornbread Cook-Off.

Prep Time: 30 minutes
(Ready in 1 hour 10 minutes)

FILLING
1	lb. smoked sausage
½	cup chopped onion
1	to 2 garlic cloves, minced
2	(15-oz.) cans black-eyed peas, drained
1	(14½-oz.) can ready-to-serve fat-free chicken broth with ⅓ less sodium
1	(10-oz.) pkg. frozen chopped collard greens, thawed
	teaspoon hot pepper sauce

TOPPING
2	cups Martha White® Self-Rising Corn Meal Mix
1⅓	cups buttermilk*
2	oz. (½ cup) shredded Cheddar cheese
¼	cup finely chopped fresh parsley or cilantro
¼	cup oil
1	egg, beaten
2	teaspoons sugar

1. Heat oven to 400°F. Cut sausage in half lengthwise; cut crosswise into ¼-inch slices. In 12-inch cast iron or ovenproof skillet, combine sausage, onion and garlic; cook until sausage is browned and onion is tender, stirring occasionally.

2. Add all remaining filling ingredients; mix well. Bring to a boil. Reduce heat to low; simmer 10 minutes.

3. In large bowl, combine all topping ingredients; stir until smooth. Spoon and spread batter over sausage mixture in skillet.

4. Bake at 400°F. for 30 to 40 minutes or until golden brown. If desired, garnish with sour cream, pickled jalapeño chile slices and fresh parsley or cilantro leaves.

Yield: 8 servings

TIP: * To substitute for buttermilk, use 4 teaspoons vinegar or lemon juice plus milk to make 1⅓ cups.

Chicken and Dressing Skillet Bake

Reminiscent of Sunday dinner, this skillet dish, created by Sue Gulledge of Springville, Alabama, took top honors in the 1997 National Cornbread Cook-Off.

Prep Time: 25 minutes (Ready in 1 hour)

2	tablespoons butter or margarine
1	cup chopped onions
1	cup chopped celery
1	tablespoon oil
3	cups cubed cooked chicken
1	cup frozen whole kernel corn
2	(6-oz.) pkg. Martha White® Cotton Pickin' or Buttermilk Cornbread Mix
1½	teaspoons poultry seasoning
1¾	cups milk
2	eggs, beaten

1. Heat oven to 400°F. Melt butter in 10-inch cast iron or ovenproof skillet over medium heat. Add onions and celery; cook 8 to 10 minutes or until tender, stirring occasionally. Spoon onions and celery into large bowl.

2. Add oil to same skillet; place in oven to heat for 5 minutes. Add all remaining ingredients to onions and celery in bowl; blend well. Pour batter over oil in hot skillet.

3. Bake at 400°F. for 29 to 35 minutes or until golden brown. Cut into wedges. Garnish with fresh sage leaves and serve with chicken gravy, if desired.

Yield: 6 servings

Chicken and Dressing Skillet Bake

Perfect Gravy

CREAM GRAVY

Good Southern cooks know how to make good gravy. If you aspire to be included in this elite group, there is a secret to success. Good cream gravy always starts with drippings from pan-frying sausage, bacon, chicken or pork chops. Your gravy will always turn out just right if you use equal parts of drippings and flour. The basic proportions are ¼ cup drippings to ¼ cup flour to 2 cups milk. Follow the directions on page 108, remember these proportions, and you'll be able to make perfect gravy no matter what the drippings.

RED EYE GRAVY

Red Eye Gravy isn't really gravy at all. It's "Southern au jus" made from the browned bits left in the skillet after frying country ham. Some folks just add water to the hot skillet. Others insist on adding water and little coffee for color.

Seven Supper Ideas for Seven Days

Sunday—Chicken and Dressing Skillet Bake, page 104

Monday—Smoky White Bean Stew with Corn Meal Dumplings, page 80

Tuesday—Country Italian Sausage Pie, page 87

Wednesday—-Beans and Greens under Cornbread, page 98

Thursday—Chicken à la King Pot Pie, page 88

Friday—Chili Dog Pie, page 94

Saturday—Country Breakfast Cobbler, page 86

Black-Eyed Pea Cornbread Skillet

Turn a skillet of cornbread into a hearty main dish by adding peas, cooked ground beef, cream-style corn and cheese. The combination was inspired by Kathleen Davis of Millport, Alabama, a semi-finalist in the 1998 National Cornbread Cook-Off.

Prep Time: 25 minutes (Ready in 55 minutes)

- 1 lb. ground beef
- 1 medium onion, chopped
- ½ teaspoon salt
- 1 cup Martha White® Self-Rising Corn Meal Mix
- ¾ cup buttermilk*
- ¼ cup oil
- 2 eggs, beaten
- 1 (15-oz.) can black-eyed peas, drained
- 1 (8.5-oz.) can cream-style corn
- 4 oz. (1 cup) shredded Cheddar cheese
- 2 tablespoons chopped pickled jalapeño chiles

1. Heat oven to 400°F. In 10-inch cast iron skillet, cook ground beef, onion and salt over medium-high heat until beef is thoroughly cooked and onion is tender. Drain. Wipe skillet clean with paper towel; spray with nonstick cooking spray.

2. In large bowl, combine corn meal mix, buttermilk, oil and eggs; blend well. Stir in black-eyed peas, corn, cheese, chiles and ground beef mixture. Pour batter into sprayed skillet.

3. Bake at 400°F. for 20 to 30 minutes or until golden brown and set.

Yield: 10 servings

TIP: * To substitute for buttermilk, use 2¼ teaspoons vinegar or lemon juice plus milk to make ¾ cup.

Black-Eyed Pea Cornbread Skillet

Grandma's Sunday Fried Chicken and Gravy

Prep Time: 1 hour

CHICKEN

   1 cup Martha White® All Purpose Flour
   1 teaspoon salt
   ½ teaspoon pepper
   3 to 3½ lb. cut-up frying chicken
     Oil or shortening for frying
1½ cups water

GRAVY

   ¼ cup drippings from chicken
   ¼ cup Martha White® All Purpose Flour
   2 cups milk
     Salt and pepper

1. In a large plastic bag, combine 1 cup flour, 1 teaspoon salt and ½ teaspoon pepper; mix well. Add chicken, 1 or 2 pieces at a time; shake to coat.

2. In large skillet, heat ½ inch oil over medium heat to 350°F. Add chicken; cover and fry for 20 to 25 minutes or until golden brown and crisp, turning every 10 minutes.

3. Remove chicken from skillet; pour off drippings and reserve for gravy. Return chicken to skillet. Add water. Reduce heat to medium-low; cover and cook 10 to 15 minutes or until chicken is fork-tender and juices run clear.

4. Meanwhile, in medium skillet, combine drippings from chicken and ¼ cup flour; cook and stir over medium heat about 1 minute or until thickened. Gradually stir in milk. Bring to a boil, stirring constantly. Reduce heat to low; simmer 2 to 3 minutes, stirring constantly. Add salt and pepper to taste. Serve gravy with chicken.

Yield: 6 servings

Sausage Brunch Bake

Patricia Reese, of Whitwell, Tennessee, went home $200 richer from the 1998 National Cornbread Cook-Off for this quiche-style cornbread bake.

Prep Time: 30 minutes (Ready in 1 hour)

   1 lb. bulk pork sausage
   1 small onion, chopped
   ½ cup chopped green bell pepper
   2 (6-oz.) pkg. Martha White®
     Buttermilk or Cotton Pickin'
     Cornbread Mix
1⅓ cups milk
   3 eggs, beaten
   4 oz. (1 cup) shredded Cheddar cheese

1. Heat oven to 400°F. In 10-inch cast iron or ovenproof skillet, cook sausage, onion and bell pepper over medium heat until sausage is thoroughly cooked and vegetables are tender.

2. Remove mixture from skillet. Drain. Wipe skillet clean with paper towel; spray skillet with nonstick cooking spray.

3. In medium bowl, combine cornbread mix and milk; stir until smooth. Pour half of batter into sprayed skillet. Spoon sausage mixture over batter. Pour beaten eggs over sausage. Sprinkle cheese over eggs. Spoon remaining batter over cheese.

4. Bake at 400°F. for 25 to 30 minutes or until golden brown and set.

Yield: 8 servings

Sausage Brunch Bake

World Grits Festival

St. George, South Carolina

Each Spring, thousands of grits lovers converge on St. George, South Carolina, for the World Grits Festival. Visitors eat grits, crown the Grits Queen, visit a working gristmill and cheer at the Grits Parade.

It's not surprising St. George hosts the celebration since South Carolina boasts the highest per capita consumption of grits in the country. In area supermarkets, the grits section takes up half an aisle.

Grits are simply good eating. Martha White Foods, producer of Jim Dandy® Grits, has hosted the festival's recipe contest for years.

Check out Rio Grande Grits Casserole, shown here, Grits Yorkshire Pudding in the Side Dishes chapter on page 128 and Grits Cream in the Shortcake, Desserts & Party Snacks chapter on page 210. They're all Grand-Prize winners and Martha White Kitchens favorites.

Rio Grande Grits Casserole

Prep Time: 30 minutes (Ready in 55 minutes)

4	cups water
1	cup Jim Dandy® Quick Grits
1	teaspoon garlic salt
½	lb. smoked sausage or kielbasa
1	tablespoon oil
1	cup chopped onions
1	cup chopped green bell pepper
2	garlic cloves, minced
1¾	cups salsa
1	(15-oz.) can black beans, drained
8	oz. (2 cups) shredded Cheddar cheese
	Sour cream, if desired
	Finely chopped fresh cilantro, if desired

1. Heat oven to 350°F. Grease 13x9-inch (3-quart) baking dish. In large saucepan, bring water to a boil. Gradually stir in grits and garlic salt. Reduce heat to low; cover and cook 5 to 7 minutes or until thickened, stirring occasionally.

2. Cut sausage in half lengthwise; cut crosswise into ¼-inch slices. Heat oil in large skillet over medium-high heat until hot. Add sausage, onions, bell pepper and garlic; cook until sausage is browned and vegetables are tender, stirring occasionally.

3. Stir in salsa and black beans; cook until thoroughly heated. Spoon half of grits mixture into greased baking dish. Top with half of sausage mixture and 1 cup of the cheese. Repeat layers with remaining ingredients.

4. Bake at 350°F. for 20 to 25 minutes or until thoroughly heated. Serve with sour cream and cilantro.

Yield: 8 servings

Rio Grande Grits Casserole

Crispy Fried Fish

The secret to crispy fried fish is to roll it in seasoned corn meal before you fry it. It's a winner for catfish, crappie and brim.

Prep Time: 25 minutes

Oil for frying
1 **egg**
2 **tablespoons water**
1 **cup Martha White® Self-Rising Corn Meal Mix**
¼ **teaspoon pepper**
1 **lb. fresh or frozen fish fillets, thawed**

1. In large skillet, heat 1 inch oil over medium heat to 350°F. In shallow bowl, combine egg and water; beat well. In medium bowl, combine corn meal mix and pepper; mix well.

2. Coat each fillet with corn meal mixture. Dip in egg mixture; coat again with corn meal mixture. Fry fillets in hot oil until golden brown. Drain on paper towels.

Yield: 4 servings

Pot Likker

"Pot likker" is the broth created when greens or beans are boiled in salted water that's flavored with a ham hock or bacon drippings. Glamorous it's not, but this treasured delicacy has sustained the thrifty and the hungry for generations. When the last of the pintos or turnip greens are gone, the remaining "pot likker" spooned over a hunk of crispy cornbread makes a meal in itself.

Sautéed Shrimp with Grits

Prep Time: 30 minutes

GRITS
1½ **cups chicken broth**
1½ **cups milk**
¾ **cup Jim Dandy® Quick Grits**
¼ **teaspoon salt**
4 **oz. (1 cup) shredded Cheddar cheese**
SHRIMP
1 **cup diced bacon**
1 **lb. fresh uncooked medium shrimp, shelled, deveined**
½ **cup thinly sliced green bell pepper**
½ **cup thinly sliced red bell pepper**
½ **cup thinly sliced onion**
2 **teaspoons hot pepper sauce**
Sliced green onions, if desired
Shredded Cheddar cheese, if desired

1. In large saucepan, bring chicken broth and milk to a boil. Gradually stir in grits and salt. Reduce heat to low; cover and cook 5 to 7 minutes or until thickened, stirring occasionally. Stir in Cheddar cheese. Cover to keep warm.

2. In large skillet, cook bacon over medium heat until crisp. Remove bacon from skillet; drain on paper towels. Reserve 2 tablespoons drippings in skillet.

3. Add shrimp, bell peppers and onion to drippings in skillet; cook until vegetables are crisp-tender and shrimp turn pink, stirring occasionally. Add cooked bacon and hot pepper sauce.

4. Serve shrimp mixture over warm grits. Garnish with sliced green onions and additional Cheddar cheese.

Yield: 6 servings

Sautéed Shrimp with Grits

National Cornbread Festival and National Cornbread Cook-Off

South Pittsburg, Tennessee

Every year, folks come from miles around to South Pittsburg, on the banks of the Tennessee River, for the National Cornbread Festival. The National Cornbread Cook-Off, sponsored by Martha White Foods and Lodge Cast Iron, is the festival's centerpiece. In the middle of town, you'll find the Cook-Off pavilion where 10 lucky finalists wield well-seasoned, cast-iron pots and skillets to bake up their main-dish creations. The Cook-Off is a testament to cornbread's versatility—and to its esteemed status in the South. Winning creations include recipes such as Chicken and Dressing Skillet Bake, page 104, and Chili Dog Pie, page 94.

SOUTH PITTSBURG, TENNESSEE

Apple Sausage Shortcakes

A quick sauté of sausage and apples turns biscuits into a breakfast shortcake.

Prep Time: 30 minutes

SHORTCAKES
> **Easy Rich Biscuit Shortcakes (page 201)**

FILLING AND TOPPING
- 1 **(10- to 12-oz.) pkg. pork sausage links, cut into 1-inch pieces**
- 3 **large Golden Delicious apples, peeled, coarsely chopped**
- ½ **cup pure maple or maple-flavored syrup**
> **Warm pure maple or maple-flavored syrup, if desired**

1. Prepare and bake shortcakes as directed in recipe.

2. Meanwhile, in large skillet, cook sausage over medium heat until browned, turning occasionally. Drain. Stir in apples; cook 5 minutes or until tender, stirring occasionally.

3. Stir in ½ cup maple syrup. Split shortcakes; fill and top with sausage mixture. Serve with additional warm maple syrup.

Yield: 8 servings

Sweet Onion Swiss Pizza

Prep Time: 45 minutes

- 1 **tablespoon olive oil**
- 2 **cups thinly sliced onions**
- 1 **(6.5-oz.) pkg. Martha White® Pizza Crust Mix**
- ½ **cup hot water**
- 1 **teaspoon olive oil**
- 3 **oz. Swiss cheese, thinly sliced, cut into 1-inch pieces**
- 1 **tablespoon chopped fresh parsley**

1. Place oven rack in lowest rack position in oven. Heat oven to 500°F. Grease large cookie sheet or pizza pan. Heat 1 tablespoon olive oil in medium skillet over medium heat until hot. Add onions; cook 5 to 8 minutes or until tender, stirring occasionally. Cool slightly.

2. In medium bowl, combine pizza crust mix and hot water. Stir vigorously with fork about 30 strokes or until blended. Shape dough into ball; coat with 1 teaspoon olive oil. Cover; let rise in warm place (80 to 85°F.) for 5 minutes.

3. With greased hands, press dough into a 9-inch round on greased cookie sheet. Pinch edge to form rim. Sprinkle cheese and onions over dough; sprinkle with parsley.

4. Bake at 500°F. on lowest oven rack for 12 to 14 minutes or until crust is golden brown and cheese is melted. Let stand 5 minutes before serving.

Yield: 8 servings

Sausage and Sweet Pepper Calzone

Prep Time: 30 minutes (Ready in 55 minutes)

- ½ **lb. bulk pork sausage**
- 2 **cups thin onion wedges**
- 1 **cup green bell pepper strips**
- 1 **cup red bell pepper strips**
- 1 **(6.5-oz.) pkg. Martha White® Pizza Crust Mix**
- ½ **cup hot water**
- 1 **teaspoon oil**
- 6 **oz. (1½ cups) shredded Swiss cheese**
- 1 **egg, beaten**

1. Heat oven to 375°F. Grease large cookie sheet. In large skillet, combine sausage, onions and bell peppers; cook over medium-high heat until sausage is browned, stirring occasionally. Drain.

2. In medium bowl, combine pizza crust mix and hot water. Stir vigorously with fork about 30 strokes or until blended. Shape dough into ball; coat with oil. Cover; let rise in warm place (80 to 85°F.) for 5 minutes.

3. On floured surface, roll out dough to 14-inch oval. Place on greased cookie sheet. Spoon sausage mixture on half of dough to within ½ inch of edge. Sprinkle with cheese. Drizzle with beaten egg. Fold dough over filling. Brush edge of dough with water; press to seal.

4. Bake at 375°F. for 20 to 25 minutes or until golden brown. Cool 10 minutes before serving.

Yield: 10 servings

Side Dish

The phrase "side dishes" is an unfortunate misnomer that lessens the importance of this recipe category. In the South, dishes such as fried okra, sliced ripe tomatoes, turnip greens, butter beans, cheese grits and cornbread dressing enjoy a heap of respect and are as important on the plate as the meat. Of course, there's strength in numbers. Governed by what's in the garden, the traditional spread usually includes from three to five side dishes. And every Southerner knows the cornbread dressing outweighs the turkey in holiday significance. So when company's coming for dinner, don't prepare more pot roast, just add another side dish.

Georgia Pecan and Dried Apple Cornbread Dressing, page 118

To Stuff or To Dress…

The words "stuffing" and "dressing" mean essentially the same thing, but regional preferences often separate along the Mason-Dixon line. Most Southerners don't stuff, they dress. Traditional dressing includes cornbread and is usually baked in a separate pan. Why, is a mystery. It must have something to do with baked cornbread dressing's irresistible, buttery crispness. In the South, cornbread dressing is not relegated to the holidays, but is enjoyed year 'round with roast chicken.

Georgia Pecan and Dried Apple Cornbread Dressing at right.

Georgia Pecan and Dried Apple Cornbread Dressing

Prep Time: 30 minutes
(Ready in 1 hour 55 minutes)

	Southern Cornbread (page 24)
½	**cup butter or margarine**
2	**medium onions, chopped**
4	**cups dry bread cubes or crumbled, toasted biscuits**
1	**cup chopped pecans, toasted***
1	**cup raisins or sweetened dried cranberries**
1	**(6-oz.) pkg. dried apple chunks, chopped, or 1 medium apple, chopped**
1½	**cups apple juice**
2	**(14½-oz.) cans ready-to-serve chicken broth**

1. Prepare cornbread as directed. Cool 15 minutes. Crumble cornbread to make 6 cups. Set aside.

2. Heat oven to 375°F. Grease 13x9-inch (3-quart) baking dish or pan. Melt butter in large skillet over medium heat. Add onions; cook until tender, stirring occasionally.

3. In large bowl, combine onions, crumbled cornbread and all remaining ingredients; mix well. Spoon into greased baking dish.

4. Bake at 375°F. for 40 to 45 minutes or until golden brown.

Yield: 12 servings

TIP: * To toast pecans, spread on cookie sheet. Bake at 350°F. for 5 to 7 minutes or until golden brown, stirring occasionally.

Classic Martha White Cornbread Dressing

A company-sized recipe that has been a holiday and Sunday-dinner favorite for generations.

**Prep Time: 20 minutes
(Ready in 1 hour 10 minutes)**

	Southern Cornbread (page 24) **Martha White Hot Rize® Biscuits (page 9) or toasted dry bread cubes**
½	cup butter or margarine
1	cup chopped onions
1	cup chopped celery
½	cup chopped fresh parsley
2	teaspoons dried sage leaves
½	teaspoon dried thyme leaves
½	teaspoon pepper
4	cups chicken broth

1. Prepare cornbread and biscuits as directed. Cool 15 minutes. Crumble cornbread to make 6 cups; crumble biscuits to make 4 cups. Set aside.

2. Heat oven to 375°F. Grease 13x9-inch (3-quart) baking dish or pan. Melt butter in large skillet over medium-high heat. Add onions and celery; cook until tender, stirring occasionally.

3. In large bowl, combine onion mixture, crumbled cornbread and biscuits, and all remaining ingredients; mix well. Spoon into greased baking dish.

4. Bake at 375°F. for 45 to 50 minutes or until golden brown.

Yield: 12 servings

Traditional Sage Cornbread Dressing

Eggs add moisture to this traditional dressing.

Prep Time: 30 minutes (Ready in 1 hour)

	Southern Cornbread (page 24)
⅓	cup butter or margarine
1	cup chopped celery
½	cup chopped onion
2½	cups crumbled, toasted biscuits or dry bread crumbs
1	teaspoon dried sage leaves
½	teaspoon pepper
3	cups chicken broth
2	eggs, beaten

1. Prepare cornbread as directed. Cool 15 minutes. Crumble cornbread to make 6 cups. Set aside.

2. Heat oven to 450°F. Grease 13x9-inch (3-quart) baking dish or pan. Melt butter in medium skillet over medium-high heat. Add celery and onion; cook until tender, stirring occasionally.

3. In large bowl, combine celery mixture, crumbled cornbread, bread pieces, sage and pepper; mix well. Add broth and eggs; mix well. Pour into greased baking dish.

4. Bake at 450°F. for 30 minutes or until golden brown.

Yield: 10 servings

TIP: * Follow directions for making Southern Cornbread on the Martha White® Self-Rising Corn Meal Mix package.

Chesapeake Bay Cornbread Dressing

Adding crabmeat to the cornbread dressing is a sure way to turn dinner into a special occasion.

Prep Time: 30 minutes
(Ready in 1 hour 55 minutes)

	Southern Cornbread (page 24)
½	**cup butter or margarine**
2	**medium onions, chopped**
1	**cup chopped celery**
1	**medium green bell pepper, chopped**
1	**medium yellow or red bell pepper, chopped**
2	**tablespoons Dijon mustard**
2	**teaspoons grated lemon peel**
4	**cups dry bread cubes or crumbled, toasted biscuits**
12	**oz. fresh or frozen crabmeat, thawed, flaked***
½	**cup water**
2	**(14½-oz.) cans ready-to-serve chicken broth**

1. Prepare cornbread as directed. Cool 15 minutes. Crumble cornbread to make 6 cups. Set aside.

2. Heat oven to 375°F. Grease 13x9-inch (3-quart) baking dish or pan. Melt butter in large skillet over medium heat. Add onions, celery and bell peppers; cook until vegetables are tender, stirring occasionally. Remove from heat. Add mustard and lemon peel; mix well.

3. In large bowl, combine vegetables, crumbled cornbread and all remaining ingredients; mix well. Spoon into greased baking dish.

4. Bake at 375°F. for 40 to 45 minutes or until golden brown.

Yield: 12 servings

TIP: * Two (6-oz.) cans crabmeat, drained, flaked, or 1 (12-oz.) pkg. flaked imitation crabmeat (surimi), can be substituted for the fresh or frozen crabmeat.

Breads for Supper?

Trying to decide whether to serve cornbread or biscuits with supper? There are definite opinions among Southerners about which one to choose. Cornbread is preferred with all kinds of beans, chilis and vegetable suppers. Fried chicken and beef roasts seem to taste better with hot biscuits. If you can't decide, serve a batch of Corn Meal Supper Biscuits which combines the best of both.

Chesapeake Bay Cornbread Dressing

Cornbread Sausage Dressing with Apples and Pecans

Prep Time: 20 minutes
(Ready in 1 hour 10 minutes)

	Southern Cornbread (page 24)
	Martha White Hot Rize® Biscuits (page 9)
1	lb. bulk pork sausage
1	cup chopped onions
1	cup chopped celery
2	cups chopped unpeeled Granny Smith apples
1	cup coarsely chopped pecans
½	cup chopped fresh parsley
2	teaspoons dried sage leaves
½	teaspoon dried thyme leaves
½	teaspoon pepper
4	cups chicken broth

1. Prepare cornbread and biscuits as directed. Cool 15 minutes. Crumble cornbread to make 5 cups; crumble biscuits to make 5 cups. Set aside.

2. Heat oven to 375°F. Grease 13x9-inch (3-quart) baking dish or pan. In large skillet, cook sausage, onions and celery over medium-high heat until sausage is browned and vegetables are tender, stirring occasionally.

3. In large bowl, combine sausage and vegetable mixture, crumbled cornbread and biscuits, and all remaining ingredients; mix well. Spoon into greased baking dish.

4. Bake at 375°F. for 45 to 50 minutes or until golden brown.

Yield: 12 servings

Low Country Ham and Hominy Cornbread Dressing

Prep Time: 30 minutes
(Ready in 1 hour 55 minutes)

	Southern Cornbread (page 24)
½	cup butter or margarine
2	medium onions, chopped
2	(15.5-oz.) cans golden hominy, drained
4	cups crumbled, toasted biscuits or dry bread cubes
1	cup diced cooked country ham
1	(10-oz.) pkg. frozen chopped mustard greens or kale, thawed, drained
½	to 1 teaspoon ground thyme
½	cup water
2	(14½-oz.) cans ready-to-serve fat-free chicken broth with ⅓ less sodium

1. Prepare cornbread as directed. Cool 15 minutes. Crumble cornbread to make 6 cups. Set aside.

2. Heat oven to 375°F. Grease 13x9-inch (3-quart) baking dish or pan. Melt butter in large skillet over medium heat. Add onions; cook and stir until tender.

3. In large bowl, combine onions, crumbled cornbread and all remaining ingredients; mix well. Spoon into greased baking dish.

4. Bake at 375°F. for 40 to 45 minutes or until golden brown.

Yield: 12 servings

Southwestern Cornbread Dressing

Prep Time: 45 minutes
(Ready in 1 hour 15 minutes)

	Southern Cornbread (page 24)
2½	**cups crumbled, toasted biscuits or dry bread cubes**
6	**tablespoons butter or margarine**
1	**cup chopped green onions**
2	**medium red bell peppers, roasted, peeled and chopped***
1	**(4.5-oz.) can chopped green chiles**
½	**teaspoon pepper**
2	**(14½-oz.) cans ready-to-serve beef broth**

1. Prepare cornbread and biscuits as directed. Cool 15 minutes. Crumble cornbread to make 5 cups; crumble biscuits to make 2½ cups. Set aside.

2. Heat oven to 450°F. Grease 13x9-inch (3-quart) baking dish or pan. Melt butter in large skillet over medium-high heat. Add onions; cook until tender, stirring occasionally.

3. In large bowl, combine onions, crumbled cornbread and biscuits, and all remaining ingredients; mix well. Spoon into greased baking dish.

4. Bake at 450°F. for 30 minutes or until golden brown.

Yield: 8 servings

TIP: * To roast red bell peppers, remove stem and seeds; cut into quarters. Place, skin side up, on foil-covered cookie sheet or broiler pan. Brush lightly with oil. Broil 4 to 6 inches from heat until pepper skin is blistered and blackened. Place peppers in plastic bag; seal tightly. Place in freezer for about 15 minutes. Remove from freezer. With fingers or small knife, gently peel skin off peppers. Or bell peppers can be diced and cooked with green onions instead of roasting.

Beans and Peas

Most Southerners consider a pot of beans simmered with a ham hock and a cast iron skillet of crusty cornbread to be two of life's greatest pleasures.

More than 20 varieties of peas and beans are enjoyed in the South. In the summer when fresh peas and beans are in abundance, they are offered as side dishes. The dried varieties, often served in lieu of meat during fall and winter, have kept generations of Southern stomachs satisfied. Preferred varieties are dictated by family and regional customs. White beans are popular in Tennessee; many Alabamians consider black-eyes the pea of choice; red beans rule in Louisiana; and, farther west, pintos reign. Here are just some of the many choices available in the South:

> white beans
>
> pinto beans
>
> black-eyed peas
>
> crowder peas
>
> purple hull peas
>
> speckled butter beans
>
> pole beans
>
> field peas
>
> shelly beans
>
> red beans
>
> butter beans
>
> lima beans
>
> sweet peas
>
> cow peas
>
> cranberry beans
>
> lady peas
>
> leather britches

Weekday Supper Cornbread Dressing

This makes just the right amount of dressing for a small family, and it starts with a convenient cornbread mix.

Prep Time: 45 minutes
(Ready in 1 hour 15 minutes)

 1 **(6-oz.) pkg. Martha White® Cotton Pickin' or Buttermilk Cornbread Mix**
 2 **tablespoons butter or margarine**
 ½ **cup chopped celery**
 ¼ **cup chopped onion**
 ¼ **teaspoon ground sage or poultry seasoning**
 ¼ **teaspoon pepper**
 ¾ **cup chicken broth**
 1 **egg, beaten**

1. Prepare and bake cornbread as directed on package. Cool 15 minutes. Coarsely crumble cornbread into large bowl. Set aside.

2. Heat oven to 350°F. Grease 8-inch square (2-quart) baking dish or pan. Melt butter in medium skillet over medium-high heat. Add celery and onion; cook until tender, stirring occasionally. Add to cornbread in bowl. Add all remaining ingredients; mix well. Pour into greased baking dish.

3. Bake at 350°F. for 25 to 30 minutes or until golden brown.

Yield: 5 servings

Cajun Cornbread Dressing

Prep Time: 20 minutes
(Ready in 1 hour 10 minutes)

   Southern Cornbread (page 24)
   Martha White Hot Rize® Biscuits (page 9) or toasted dry bread cubes
 1 **lb. andouille or smoked sausage, cut into bite-sized pieces**
 2 **cups chopped onions**
 1 **cup chopped celery**
 1 **large red bell pepper, chopped**
 2 **garlic cloves, minced**
 ½ **cup chopped fresh parsley**
 ½ **teaspoon dried thyme leaves**
 ½ **teaspoon pepper**
 ¼ **teaspoon crushed red pepper flakes**
 4 **cups chicken broth**

1. Prepare cornbread and biscuits as directed. Cool 15 minutes. Crumble cornbread to make 6 cups; crumble biscuits to make 5 cups. Set aside.

2. Heat oven to 375°F. Grease 13x9-inch (3-quart) baking dish or pan. In large skillet, cook sausage, onions, celery, bell pepper and garlic over medium-high heat until sausage is browned and vegetables are tender, stirring occasionally.

3. In large bowl, combine sausage and vegetable mixture, crumbled cornbread and biscuits, and all remaining ingredients; mix well. Spoon into greased baking dish.

4. Bake at 375°F. for 45 to 50 minutes or until golden brown.

Yield: 12 servings

Cajun Cornbread Dressing

Cheese Grits Casserole

**Prep Time: 30 minutes
(Ready in 1 hour 30 minutes)**

4	cups water
1	teaspoon salt
1	cup Jim Dandy® Quick Grits
6	oz. (1½ cups) shredded sharp Cheddar cheese
½	cup butter or margarine
1	cup milk
4	eggs, beaten
¼	teaspoon ground red pepper (cayenne)

1. Heat oven to 350°F. Grease 2-quart casserole. In large saucepan, combine water and salt. Bring to a boil. Gradually stir in grits. Reduce heat to low; cover and cook 5 minutes, stirring occasionally.

2. Remove from heat. Add 1 cup of the cheese and the butter; stir until melted. Add milk, eggs and pepper; mix well. Pour mixture into greased casserole. Sprinkle with remaining ½ cup cheese.

3. Bake at 350°F. for 1 hour or until golden brown. Let stand 10 minutes before serving.

Yield: 8 servings

Garlic Cheese Grits Casserole

Prep Time: 15 minutes (Ready in 1 hour)

4	cups water
1	teaspoon salt
1	cup Jim Dandy® Quick Grits
8	oz. (2 cups) shredded sharp Cheddar cheese
½	cup butter or margarine
½	teaspoon garlic powder
3	eggs, beaten
1	tablespoon Worcestershire sauce

1. Heat oven to 350°F. Grease 2-quart casserole. In large saucepan, combine water and salt. Bring to a boil. Gradually stir in grits. Reduce heat to low; cover and cook 5 minutes, stirring occasionally.

2. Remove from heat. Stir in Cheddar cheese, butter and garlic powder; stir until cheese is melted. Add eggs and Worcestershire sauce; mix well. Pour mixture into greased casserole. Sprinkle with paprika, if desired.

3. Bake at 350°F. for 40 to 45 minutes or until set. Let stand 10 minutes before serving.

Yield: 8 servings

Country Grits Casserole

Prep Time: 30 minutes
(Ready in 1 hour 30 minutes)

1	**lb. bulk pork sausage**
4	**cups water**
½	**teaspoon salt**
1	**cup Jim Dandy® Quick Grits**
6	**oz. (1½ cups) shredded sharp Cheddar cheese**
¼	**cup butter or margarine**
½	**cup milk**
4	**eggs, beaten**

1. Heat oven to 350°F. Grease 3-quart casserole. In large skillet, cook sausage over medium heat until browned, stirring occasionally. Drain.

2. Meanwhile, in large saucepan, combine water and salt. Bring to a boil. Gradually stir in grits. Reduce heat to low; cover and cook 5 minutes, stirring occasionally.

3. Remove from heat. Add 1 cup of the cheese and the butter; stir until melted. Add milk, eggs and cooked sausage; mix well. Pour mixture into greased casserole. Sprinkle with remaining ½ cup cheese.

4. Bake at 350°F. for 1 hour or until golden brown. Let stand 10 minutes before serving.

Yield: 8 servings

Grits with Artichokes and Bacon

This delicious combination of flavors made Eileen Watson of Oviedo, Florida, a winner at the World Grits Festival Recipe Contest.

Prep Time: 30 minutes
(Ready in 1 hour 15 minutes)

6	**slices bacon**
2	**(14½-oz.) cans ready-to-serve chicken broth**
	Water
1	**cup Jim Dandy® Quick Grits**
1	**cup grated Parmesan cheese**
3	**tablespoons sour cream**
2	**tablespoons butter or margarine**
1	**garlic clove, minced**
½	**teaspoon ground red pepper (cayenne)**
1	**(14-oz.) can artichoke hearts, drained, coarsely chopped**
2	**eggs, beaten**

1. Heat oven to 375°F. Grease 8-inch square (2-quart) baking dish. In large skillet, cook bacon over medium heat until crisp. Drain on paper towels. Crumble.

2. In measuring cup, combine broth and enough water to make 4 cups. Pour into large saucepan. Bring to a boil. Gradually stir in grits. Reduce heat to low; cover and cook 5 minutes, stirring occasionally.

3. Remove from heat. Add crumbled bacon and all remaining ingredients; mix well. Pour into greased baking dish.

4. Bake at 375°F. for 45 minutes or until set.

Yield: 8 servings

Great Grits

Few foods stir up as much passion as grits. Yet, along with the familiar buttermilk biscuit, they symbolize Southern cooking.

What are Grits?

Some historians claim grits are America's first food, offered by Native Americans to the settlers who landed in Jamestown, Virginia, in 1607.

Grits are related to corn meal, since both are made from dried corn. Grits are just more coarsely ground than corn meal. White grits made from white corn are the most familiar, however, yellow grits made from yellow corn are also available.

Whole ground grits are made by grinding the whole corn kernel, including the bran, germ and hard starchy endosperm. Often very coarsely ground, these grits may take more than 30 minutes to cook. Quick and regular grits, the two most popular types, cook much more quickly. They're made by tempering dried corn, removing the bran and germ, then grinding the hard starchy endosperm. Quick grits cook in 5 to 10 minutes, however many grits lovers prefer to simmer them longer, adding water as needed. The grits become creamier, but never lose their characteristic texture. Instant grits are cooked and dehydrated before packaging and are prepared by just adding hot water.

Grits are traditionally served as a breakfast side dish with butter and black pepper. In fact, many Southerners don't consider the morning meal breakfast without them.

Grits Yorkshire Pudding

Bake this pudding in a skillet and serve it with roast beef, says Diane Fletcher of Hernando, Mississippi. She won the Grand Prize for it at the 1992 World Grits Festival Recipe Contest.

Prep Time: 30 minutes (Ready in 50 minutes)

2	cups roast beef drippings
1½	cups water
1½	cups milk
¾	cup Jim Dandy® Quick Grits
¼	teaspoon salt
⅔	cup Martha White® Self-Rising Flour
⅔	cup milk
1	egg, beaten

1. Heat oven to 425°F. Pour beef drippings into 9-inch cast iron or ovenproof skillet. Place in oven to heat.

2. Meanwhile, in large saucepan, combine water and 1½ cups milk. Bring to a boil. Gradually stir in grits and salt; return to a boil. Reduce heat to low; cover and cook 5 minutes, stirring occasionally. Cool slightly.

3. Add flour, ⅔ cup milk and egg; mix well. Remove hot skillet from oven. Pour grits mixture over beef drippings.

4. Bake at 425°F. for 20 minutes or until golden brown. Serve pudding with beef roast.

Yield: 8 servings

Fried Grits Slices

Prep Time: 20 minutes
(Ready in 2 hours 20 minutes)

 4 cups water
 1 teaspoon salt
 1 cup Jim Dandy® Quick Grits
   Martha White® Self-Rising or
     All Purpose Flour
   Oil or shortening for frying

1. Grease 8x4-inch loaf pan. In large saucepan, combine water and salt. Bring to a boil. Gradually stir in grits. Reduce heat to low; cover and cook 5 minutes, stirring occasionally. Pour grits into greased pan. Cool slightly. Cover; refrigerate 2 hours or until firm.

2. Remove grits from pan; place on cutting board. Cut into ½-inch slices. Place flour in shallow bowl; add slices. Turn to coat all sides.

3. In large skillet, heat ¼ inch oil over medium heat to 350°F. Fry grits slices, a few at a time, until golden brown on both sides. Drain on paper towels.

Yield: 12 slices

Polenta

Prep Time: 45 minutes
(Ready in 1 hour 45 minutes)

 6 tablespoons butter or margarine
 ½ cup finely chopped onion
 3 cups milk
 1 cup Martha White® Corn Meal
 1 cup water
 ¼ cup grated Parmesan cheese
 ½ teaspoon salt
 2 tablespoons butter or margarine,
     melted, or olive oil

1. Grease 9-inch square pan. Melt 6 tablespoons butter in large saucepan over medium heat. Add onion; cook until tender, stirring occasionally. Add milk; bring to a boil over medium-high heat.

2. Meanwhile, in small bowl, combine corn meal and water; mix well. With fork, stir corn meal mixture into boiling milk mixture. Reduce heat to medium; cook 15 minutes or until mixture is very thick, stirring constantly.

3. Remove from heat. Stir in cheese and salt. Spoon and spread mixture into greased pan. Cool 15 minutes. Refrigerate 1 to 2 hours or freeze 30 minutes or until firm.

4. Cut polenta into 9 squares. With pancake turner, carefully remove from pan. Brush top and bottom of squares with 2 tablespoons butter. Place squares on broiler pan; broil 4 to 6 inches from heat for 10 to 15 minutes or until hot and golden brown, turning once.

Yield: 9 servings

Old-Fashioned Corn Meal Mush

Prep Time: 30 minutes

2½ cups water
½ cup Martha White® Self-Rising Corn Meal Mix

1. In medium saucepan, bring water to a boil. With wire whisk, gradually stir in corn meal mix.

2. Reduce heat to low; cook 20 to 30 minutes or until desired consistency, stirring occasionally.

Yield: 6 servings

FRIED MUSH: Pour hot mush into lightly greased 9x5 or 8x4-inch loaf pan. Cover with plastic wrap; refrigerate at least 2 hours. Remove from pan. Cut into ¾-inch slices. Heat 2 tablespoons oil in medium skillet over medium heat until hot. Add mush slices; cook until golden brown on both sides.

Some Say Polenta, We Say Mush

Have you seen polenta popping up on trendy menus and in grocery stores nationwide? Well, polenta is just the Italian equivalent of Southern corn meal mush. In Italy, polenta is served as a side dish with meaty stews and sausages. In the South, corn meal mush is traditionally served for breakfast.

Whether you call it polenta or mush, the best way to prepare it is to chill, slice, and broil it or fry it in a skillet. Serve the crisp slices Italian-style as a supper side dish or Southern-style with a hearty country breakfast.

Peppered Parmesan Spoon Bread

Prep Time: 20 minutes
(Ready in 1 hour 10 minutes)

2 cups water
1 cup Martha White® Self-Rising Corn Meal Mix
⅓ cup grated Parmesan cheese
1 teaspoon sugar
½ teaspoon white pepper or coarse ground black pepper
2 tablespoons butter or margarine
1 cup milk
3 eggs, separated

1. Heat oven to 375°F. Grease 2-quart deep casserole or 8-cup soufflé dish. In large saucepan, bring water to a boil. Gradually stir in corn meal mix; cook until mixture is very thick and pulls away from sides of saucepan, stirring constantly.

2. Stir in cheese, sugar, pepper and butter; blend well. Add milk and egg yolks; blend well.

3. In medium bowl, beat egg whites until soft peaks form. Fold into corn meal mixture. Pour into greased casserole.

4. Bake at 375°F. for 45 to 50 minutes or until golden brown and set. Serve warm.

Yield: 8 servings

CHILE PEPPER PARMESAN SPOON BREAD: Omit white pepper. Add ¼ cup chopped roasted red peppers or 1 (4.5-oz.) can chopped green chiles, drained, just before folding in egg whites.

Chile Pepper Parmesan Spoon Bread

Fried Green Tomatoes

Prep Time: 20 minutes

- 1 (6-oz.) pkg. Martha White® Cotton Pickin' Cornbread Mix
  Salt
- 5 firm medium green tomatoes, cut into ½-inch slices
  Oil or shortening for frying

1. Place cornbread mix in shallow pan. Add salt to taste; mix well. Add tomato slices; turn to coat with mixture.

2. In large skillet, heat ¼ inch oil over medium heat to 350°F. Fry tomato slices, a few at a time, until golden brown on both sides. Drain on paper towels.

Yield: 6 servings

Old South Spoon Bread

Spoon bread is a corn meal soufflé. Separating the eggs and whipping the whites creates its characteristic puffy, light texture.

Prep Time: 15 minutes
(Ready in 1 hour 5 minutes)

- 1 cup Martha White® Self-Rising Corn Meal Mix
- 1½ cups boiling water
- 1 cup buttermilk*
- 1 tablespoon butter or margarine
- 1 teaspoon sugar
- ¼ teaspoon baking soda
- 3 eggs, separated

1. Heat oven to 375°F. Grease 1½-quart casserole. In large bowl, combine corn meal and boiling water; stir until slightly cooled.

2. Add buttermilk, butter, sugar, baking soda and egg yolks; beat well.

3. In medium bowl, beat egg whites until soft peaks form. Fold into corn meal mixture. Pour into greased casserole.

4. Bake at 375°F. for 45 to 50 minutes or until golden brown and set. Serve warm.

Yield: 8 servings

TIP: * To substitute for buttermilk, use 1 tablespoon vinegar or lemon juice plus milk to make 1 cup.

Tennessee Cornbread Salad

This hearty salad features flavorful tomatoes, bell peppers, onions and sweet pickles, all chilled with a mayonnaise and pickle juice dressing.

**Prep Time: 30 minutes
(Ready in 3 hours 30 minutes)**

- 1 **(6-oz.) pkg. Martha White® Buttermilk Cornbread Mix**
- 12 **slices bacon**
- 3 **cups chopped tomatoes**
- 1 **cup chopped green bell pepper**
- 1 **cup chopped onions**
- ½ **cup sweet pickles, chopped, reserving ¼ cup liquid**
- 1 **cup mayonnaise**

1. Prepare and bake cornbread as directed on package. Cool 1 hour or until completely cooled.

2. In large skillet, cook bacon over medium heat until crisp. Drain on paper towels. Crumble.

3. Crumble half of cornbread into bottom of large serving bowl. In another bowl, combine tomatoes, bell pepper, onions, pickles and crumbled bacon; mix well. Spoon half of vegetable mixture over cornbread.

4. In small bowl, combine mayonnaise and reserved pickle liquid; mix well. Spread half of mixture over vegetables. Repeat layering with remaining cornbread, vegetables and dressing. Cover tightly; refrigerate 2 to 3 hours before serving.

Yield: 8 servings

Tex-Mex Cornbread Salad

Prep Time: 45 minutes (3 hours 45 minutes)

- 1 **(6-oz.) pkg. Martha White® Mexican Cornbread Mix**
- 12 **slices bacon**
- 2 **(15.5-oz.) cans pinto beans, drained**
- 2 **cups chopped tomatoes**
- 1 **cup chopped green onions**
- ½ **cup chopped green bell pepper**
- ¼ **to ½ cup chopped seeded jalapeño chiles**
- 8 **oz. (2 cups) shredded Monterey Jack cheese**
- 1 **cup sour cream**
- 1 **cup salsa**
   Additional sour cream and jalapeño chile slices, if desired

1. Prepare and bake cornbread as directed on package. Cool 1 hour or until completely cooled.

2. In large skillet, cook bacon over medium heat until crisp. Drain on paper towels. Crumble.

3. Crumble half of cornbread into bottom of large serving bowl. Top with half of pinto beans. In another bowl, combine tomatoes, green onions, bell pepper and chopped jalapeño chiles; mix well. Spoon half of vegetable mixture over beans. Sprinkle with half of crumbled bacon and half of cheese.

4. In medium bowl, combine sour cream and salsa; mix well. Spread half of mixture over cheese. Repeat layering with remaining cornbread, beans, vegetables, bacon, cheese and dressing. Cover tightly; refrigerate 2 to 3 hours before serving. Garnish with sour cream and jalapeño chile slices.

Yield: 8 servings

Fried Okra

A heavy batter isn't necessary for this Southern staple. Fresh okra's flavor comes through with a simple corn meal coating.

Prep Time: 30 minutes

1	**lb. fresh okra, trimmed**
¾	**cup Martha White® Self-Rising Corn Meal Mix**
	Oil or shortening for frying

1. Cut okra crosswise into ½-inch slices. In resealable food storage plastic bag, combine okra and corn meal mix; shake to coat evenly.

2. In large skillet, heat ¼ inch oil over medium heat to 350°F. Fry okra in hot oil until crisp and golden brown, stirring occasionally. Drain on paper towels.

Yield: 4 servings

Summer Squash and Cornbread Casserole

Forget cracker crumbs—a crown of crispy cornbread is just what buttery summer squash needs. For the ideal summer vegetable supper, serve this casserole with sliced tomatoes and simmered green beans.

Prep Time: 40 minutes

¼	**cup butter or margarine**
1	**large sweet onion, cut into thin wedges**
2	**lb. yellow summer squash, cut into ¼-inch slices (about 8 cups)**
¼	**cup water**
½	**teaspoon salt**
¼	**teaspoon coarse ground black pepper**
1	**(6-oz.) pkg. Martha White® Cotton Pickin' or Buttermilk Cornbread Mix**
⅔	**cup milk**
2	**oz. (½ cup) shredded Cheddar cheese**

1. Heat oven to 450°F. Grease 2-quart casserole. Melt butter in large skillet over medium-high heat. Add onion; cook until tender, stirring occasionally. Add squash, water, salt and pepper. Reduce heat; cover and cook 15 minutes or until squash is tender.

2. With fork, mash squash gently to break up large pieces. Cook, uncovered, for 5 minutes or until slightly thickened and creamy. Pour into greased baking dish.

3. In medium bowl, combine cornbread mix and milk; mix well. Stir in cheese. Spoon batter around edge of mixture in casserole.

4. Bake at 450°F. for 15 to 18 minutes or until cornbread is golden brown. Let stand 5 minutes before serving.

Yield: 8 servings

Summer Squash and Cornbread Casserole

Pies
& Cobblers

Pies and cobblers are enjoyed like no other desserts in the South. They're like old friends—inviting, informal and comfortable. Their unpretentious looks and friendly flavors can be deceiving—for no matter how sweet the peaches, how rich the custard or how fresh the pecans, every filling needs a good crust. Learning to make a good pie crust takes a little time and practice. But once mastered, this skill will serve you well for a lifetime, because every day is a good day for pie and cobbler.

Martha White Pecan Pie, page 140

Pastry for One-Crust Pie

Alice Jarman's tried-and-true method for making perfect pie crust.

Prep Time: 15 minutes

> 1 **cup Martha White® All Purpose Flour**
> ½ **teaspoon salt**
> ⅓ **cup shortening**
> 2½ **to 3 tablespoons cold water**

1. In medium bowl, combine flour and salt; mix well. With pastry blender or fork, cut in half of shortening until mixture is fine and mealy. Cut in remaining shortening until mixture is consistency of small peas. Sprinkle water over mixture; stir gently with fork until dough leaves sides of bowl. If some dry particles remain in bottom of bowl, sprinkle with about ½ teaspoon water; continue to stir with fork until particles are worked into dough. Mixture should be moist enough to form a ball but should not be sticky.

2. Shape dough into ball. Flatten to ½-inch thickness, rounding and smoothing edges. On floured surface, roll out dough to 11-inch round. Carefully roll dough around rolling pin. Unroll into 9-inch pie pan, or 9- or 10-inch tart pan. Fit evenly into pan. Do not stretch.

3. If using pie pan, fold edge under to form standing rim; flute. If using tart pan, trim pastry even with pan edge.

4. For One-Crust Filled Pie: Fill and bake as directed in pie recipe.

5. For One-Crust Baked Pie Shell (Unfilled): Heat oven to 475°F. Prick bottom and sides of pastry generously with fork. Bake at 475°F. for 8 to 10 minutes or until light golden brown. Cool on wire rack 15 minutes or until completely cooled. Continue as directed in pie recipe.

Yield: One-crust pastry

Pastry for Two-Crust Pie

Prep Time: 15 minutes

> 2 **cups Martha White® All Purpose Flour**
> 1 **teaspoon salt**
> ⅔ **cup shortening**
> 4½ **to 5 tablespoons cold water**

1. In medium bowl, combine flour and salt; mix well. With pastry blender or fork, cut in half of shortening until mixture is fine and mealy. Cut in remaining shortening until mixture is consistency of small peas. Sprinkle water over mixture; stir gently with fork until dough leaves sides of bowl. If some dry particles remain in bottom of bowl, sprinkle with about ½ teaspoon water; continue to stir with fork until particles are worked into dough. Mixture should be moist enough to form a ball but should not be sticky.

2. Shape dough into 2 balls. Flatten dough balls to ½-inch thickness, rounding and smoothing edges. On floured surface, roll out 1 ball of dough to 11-inch round. Carefully roll dough around rolling pin. Unroll into 9-inch pie pan, or 9- or 10-inch tart pan. Fit evenly into pan. Do not stretch. Trim pastry even with pan edge.

3. Roll out remaining ball of dough. Set aside. Continue as directed in pie recipe.

Yield: Two-crust pastry

Press 'n Bake
Cream Cheese Crust

This is one of the easiest crusts you can make. Its rich flavor and tender texture will entice you to make it often.

Prep Time: 10 minutes (Ready in 40 minutes)

1   (3-oz.) pkg. cream cheese, softened
½   cup butter or margarine, softened
1   cup Martha White® All Purpose Flour

1. In medium bowl, combine cream cheese and butter; beat until smooth.
Add flour; blend well. Cover with plastic wrap; refrigerate 30 minutes.

2. Press dough into bottom and up sides of 9-inch pie pan. Flute edge as desired. Fill and bake as directed in pie recipe.

Yield: One-crust pastry

The Elusive Perfect Pie Crust

Alice Jarman, the first director of the Martha White Kitchens, developed a method for making perfect pie crust. Her method is still used today in kitchens across the South.

Former Martha White Test Kitchens Director, Alice Jarman.

Flaky pie crust is the result of cutting shortening into flour in small pieces. With gentle mixing and rolling, bits of shortening remain in the dough and melt during baking to produce layers of flaky crust. Alice's secret to perfection is to cut the shortening into the flour in two steps.

For tenderness, cut half the shortening into flour in small pieces.

For flakiness, cut remaining shortening in until it's the size of small peas.

The result of this two-step method is the tender flaky pie crust that is the crowning glory of good Southern pies and cobblers.

Miss Martha's Chess Pie

Prep Time: 25 minutes
(Ready in 2 hours 10 minutes)

CRUST
> **Pastry for One-Crust Pie (page 138)**

FILLING
- 1⅓ cups sugar
- ⅓ cup butter or margarine, softened
- 3 eggs
- ⅓ cup milk
- 1 tablespoon Martha White® Self-Rising Corn Meal Mix
- 1 teaspoon vanilla
- 1 teaspoon vinegar

1. Prepare pastry as directed for *one-crust filled pie* using 9-inch pie pan.

2. Heat oven to 350°F. In medium bowl, combine sugar and butter; beat with electric mixer until light and fluffy. Add eggs 1 at a time, beating well after each addition. Add all remaining filling ingredients; beat until blended. Pour filling into crust-lined pan.

3. Bake at 350°F. for 40 to 45 minutes or until knife inserted 1 inch from center comes out clean. Pie will continue to set as it cools. Cool on wire rack for 1 hour or until completely cooled before serving. Store in refrigerator.

Yield: 8 servings

Martha White Pecan Pie

Prep Time: 20 minutes
(Ready in 2 hours 10 minutes)

CRUST
> **Pastry for One-Crust Pie (page 138)**

FILLING
- 4 eggs
- 1 cup sugar
- 1 cup light corn syrup
- ½ cup butter or margarine, melted
- 1 teaspoon vanilla
- 1 cup pecan halves

1. Prepare pastry as directed for *one-crust filled pie* using 9-inch pie pan.

2. Heat oven to 350°F. In medium bowl, beat eggs. Add sugar, corn syrup, butter and vanilla; blend well. Stir in pecans. Pour filling into crust-lined pan.

3. Bake at 350°F. for 45 to 50 minutes or until knife inserted 1 inch from center comes out clean. Cover edge of crust with strips of foil after 15 to 20 minutes of baking if necessary to prevent excessive browning. Pie will continue to set as it cools. Cool on wire rack for 1 hour or until completely cooled before serving. Store in refrigerator.

Yield: 8 servings

CHOCOLATE PECAN PIE: Use ½ cup semi-sweet chocolate chips and ½ cup coarsely chopped pecans for the 1 cup pecan halves.

Buttermilk Pie

"Making do" was the likely inspiration for this pie made from simple ingredients. It's an all-time Martha White Kitchens favorite.

Prep Time: 20 minutes
(Ready in 2 hours 5 minutes)

CRUST
      Pastry for One-Crust Pie (page 138)*
FILLING
- 1¼ cups sugar
- 2 tablespoons Martha White® Self-Rising Corn Meal Mix
- ½ cup butter or margarine, melted
- ⅓ cup buttermilk**
- 1 teaspoon vanilla
- 3 eggs, slightly beaten

1. Prepare pastry as directed for *one-crust filled pie* using 9-inch pie pan.

2. Heat oven to 350°F. In medium bowl, combine sugar and corn meal mix; mix well. Add butter, buttermilk, vanilla and eggs; blend well. Pour filling into crust-lined pan.

3. Bake at 350°F. for 40 to 45 minutes or until knife inserted 1 inch from center comes out clean. Pie will continue to set as it cools. Cool on wire rack for 1 hour or until completely cooled. Serve at room temperature or refrigerate until serving time. Store in refrigerator.

Yield: 8 servings

TIPS: * Press 'n Bake Cream Cheese Crust can be substituted for Pastry for One-Crust Pie.
** To substitute for buttermilk, use 1 teaspoon vinegar or lemon juice plus milk to make ⅓ cup.

Raisin Walnut Pie

Prep Time: 25 minutes
(Ready in 2 hours)

CRUST
      Pastry for One-Crust Pie (page 138)
FILLING
- 1 cup raisins
- 1 cup chopped walnuts
- ¼ cup firmly packed brown sugar
- 2 teaspoons grated orange peel
- ¼ teaspoon salt
- 1½ cups light corn syrup
- 1 teaspoon orange extract or vanilla
- 3 eggs

1. Prepare pastry as directed for *one-crust filled pie* using 9-inch pie pan.

2. Heat oven to 425°F. In medium bowl, combine all filling ingredients; mix well. Pour filling into crust-lined pan. Bake at 425°F. for 10 minutes.

3. Reduce oven temperature to 350°F.; bake an additional 25 to 35 minutes or until knife inserted 1 inch from edge comes out clean. (Center will be slightly soft.) Cover edge of crust with strips of foil after 15 to 20 minutes of baking to prevent excessive browning. Cool on wire rack for 1 hour or until completely cooled. Serve at room temperature or refrigerate until serving time. If desired, serve with whipped cream. Store in refrigerator.

Yield: 8 servings

Pumpkin Chess Pie

This creamy autumn favorite might well become a holiday tradition at your family gathering.

Prep Time: 20 minutes
(Ready in 2 hours 40 minutes)

CRUST
> **Press 'n Bake Cream Cheese Crust (page 139)**

FILLING
- 1⅓ cups sugar
- 6 tablespoons butter or margarine, softened
- 4 teaspoons Martha White® Self-Rising Corn Meal Mix
- ½ teaspoon salt
- ½ teaspoon cinnamon
- ¼ teaspoon ginger
- ¼ teaspoon nutmeg
- ¼ teaspoon cloves
- 1 cup canned pumpkin
- ¼ cup plus 2 tablespoons half-and-half
- 1 teaspoon vanilla
- 2 eggs

1. Prepare crust as directed in recipe.

2. Heat oven to 350°F. In medium bowl, combine sugar and butter; beat with electric mixer until light and fluffy. Add all remaining filling ingredients; beat until well blended. Pour filling into unbaked pie shell.

3. Bake at 350°F. for 45 to 50 minutes or until knife inserted 1 inch from center comes out clean. Pie will continue to set as it cools. Cool on wire rack for 1 hour or until completely cooled. Refrigerate until well chilled before serving. Serve topped with whipped cream, if desired. Store in refrigerator.

Yield: 8 servings

Old South Sweet Potato Pie

No Southern holiday or Martha White cookbook is complete without a classic sweet potato pie.

Prep Time: 25 minutes
(Ready in 2 hours 10 minutes)

CRUST
> **Pastry for One-Crust Pie (page 138)**

FILLING
- 1⅓ cups sugar
- ⅓ cup butter or margarine, softened
- 3 eggs
- 1 (17-oz.) can sweet potatoes, drained, mashed
- ⅓ cup milk
- 1 teaspoon vanilla
- ½ teaspoon cinnamon
- ½ teaspoon nutmeg
- ¼ teaspoon salt

1. Prepare pastry as directed for *one-crust filled pie* using 9-inch pie pan.

2. Heat oven to 350°F. In medium bowl, combine sugar and butter; beat with electric mixer until light and fluffy. Add eggs 1 at a time, beating well after each addition. Add all remaining filling ingredients; beat until well blended. Pour filling into crust-lined pan.

3. Bake at 350°F. for 40 to 45 minutes or until knife inserted 1 inch from center comes out clean. Pie will continue to set as it cools. Cool on wire rack for 1 hour or until completely cooled before serving. Store in refrigerator.

Yield: 8 servings

Rich Vanilla Cream Pie

Prep Time: 35 minutes
(Ready in 1 hour 50 minutes)

CRUST
    Pastry for One-Crust Pie (page 138)
FILLING
⅔ cup sugar
2 tablespoons cornstarch
1 tablespoon Martha White® All
     Purpose Flour
¼ teaspoon salt
2¼ cups milk
3 egg yolks, slightly beaten
2 tablespoons butter or margarine
1 teaspoon vanilla
MERINGUE
3 egg whites, room temperature
½ teaspoon vanilla
¼ teaspoon cream of tartar
6 tablespoons sugar

1. Prepare and bake pastry as directed for *one-crust baked pie shell* using 9-inch pie pan. Cool; set aside.

2. Heat oven to 350°F. In medium saucepan, combine ⅔ cup sugar, cornstarch, flour and salt; mix well. Gradually stir in milk. Bring to a boil over medium heat, stirring constantly. Reduce heat to medium-low; cook an additional 2 minutes, stirring constantly. Remove saucepan from heat.

3. Gradually stir 1 cup hot mixture into egg yolks; return egg yolk mixture to saucepan. Return mixture to a boil over medium-low heat; cook 2 minutes, stirring constantly. Remove saucepan from heat; stir in butter and 1 teaspoon vanilla. Pour filling into cooled baked pie shell.

4. In small bowl, combine egg whites, ½ teaspoon vanilla and cream of tartar; beat with electric mixer at medium speed until foamy and soft peaks form. Add 6 tablespoons sugar, 1 tablespoon at a time, beating at high speed until mixture forms stiff, glossy peaks and sugar is dissolved. Spoon meringue over hot filling, spreading to seal meringue to inner edge of crust to prevent shrinking.

5. Bake at 350°F. for 12 to 15 minutes or until light golden brown. Cool on wire rack for 1 hour or until completely cooled before serving. Store in refrigerator.

Yield: 8 servings

RICH BANANA CREAM PIE: Slice 2 bananas; arrange slices in bottom of baked pie shell. Pour filling over bananas.

RICH CHOCOLATE CREAM PIE: Increase sugar in filling to 1 cup. Chop 2 oz. unsweetened chocolate; add to sugar mixture in saucepan.

RICH COCONUT CREAM PIE: Stir 1 cup flaked coconut into filling with butter and vanilla. Sprinkle meringue with ⅓ cup flaked coconut. Bake pie until meringue is light golden brown and coconut is toasted.

Lemon Rub Pie

This recipe, reminiscent of an old-fashioned chess pie, provides a fresh lemon tartness.

Prep Time: 25 minutes
(Ready in 2 hours 5 minutes)

CRUST
    Pastry for One-Crust Pie (page 138)
FILLING
1¾ **cups sugar**
  2 **tablespoons Martha White®**
      Self-Rising Corn Meal Mix
  1 **tablespoon Martha White®**
      Self-Rising Flour
 ¼ **cup butter or margarine, melted**
 ¼ **cup milk**
 ¼ **cup lemon juice**
  2 **tablespoons grated lemon peel**
  4 **eggs**

1. Prepare pastry as directed for *one-crust filled pie* using 9-inch pie pan.

2. Heat oven to 375°F. In medium bowl, combine sugar, corn meal mix and flour; mix well. Add all remaining filling ingredients; beat with electric mixer at medium speed until blended and smooth. Pour filling into crust-lined pan.

3. Bake at 375°F. for 35 to 40 minutes or until knife inserted 1 inch from center comes out clean and top is golden brown. Cool on wire rack for 1 hour or until completely cooled before serving. Store in refrigerator.

Yield: 8 servings

Fudge Custard Pie

Prep Time: 20 minutes (Ready in 50 minutes)

CRUST
    Pastry for One-Crust Pie (page 138)
FILLING
1½ **cups sugar**
 ¼ **cup unsweetened cocoa**
 ½ **cup butter or margarine, melted**
  2 **teaspoons vanilla**
  3 **eggs, slightly beaten**

1. Prepare pastry as directed for *one-crust filled pie* using 9-inch pie pan.

2. Heat oven to 350°F. In medium bowl, combine sugar and cocoa; mix well. Add butter, vanilla and eggs; blend well. Pour filling into crust-lined pan.

3. Bake at 350°F. for 25 to 30 minutes or until set. Do not overbake. Serve warm or cool. Store in refrigerator.

Yield: 8 servings

Old-Fashioned Fried Peach Pies

Fried fruit pies were an original tote-along convenience food in the South.

Prep Time: 30 minutes (Ready in 3 hours)

FILLING
  1 **cup sugar**
  1 **(7-oz.) pkg. dried peaches, chopped**
  2 **cups water**
 ¼ **cup butter or margarine**
  1 **tablespoon lemon juice**
 ½ **teaspoon cinnamon**
 ¼ **teaspoon almond extract**

CRUST
    Pastry for Two-Crust Pie (page 138)

    Oil or shortening for frying
    Powdered sugar, if desired

1. In large saucepan, combine sugar, peaches and water. Bring to a boil over medium heat. Reduce heat to low; cover and simmer 1½ hours or until tender, stirring occasionally.

2. Mash peach mixture thoroughly. Add butter, lemon juice, cinnamon and almond extract; mix well. Cool 1 hour or until completely cooled.

3. Prepare pastry for *two-crust pie* as directed. Cut dough into 10 pieces. Roll each piece into 6-inch round. Place 2 tablespoons filling in center of each round. Fold top half of round over bottom half. Brush edges with water. Press to seal. Crimp edges with fork.

4. In large skillet, heat ¼ inch oil over medium-high heat to 375°F. Fry pies, 2 at a time, on both sides until golden brown. Drain on paper towels. Cool slightly before serving; filling will be hot. Before serving, lightly sprinkle with powdered sugar. Serve warm or cool.

Yield: 10 pies

Easy Apple Pie Foldover

Prep Time: 25 minutes
(Ready in 1 hour 20 minutes)

1½   **cups (2 medium) thinly sliced, peeled apples**
¼   **cup firmly packed brown sugar**
1   **tablespoon water**
1   **teaspoon lemon juice**
1   **tablespoon Martha White® All Purpose Flour**

1   **tablespoon sugar**
¼   **teaspoon salt**
½   **teaspoon vanilla**
1   **tablespoon margarine or butter**
    Pastry for One-Crust Pie (page 138)
1   **tablespoon water**
1   **egg**

1. In medium saucepan, combine apples, brown sugar, 1 tablespoon water and lemon juice. Cook over medium heat until bubbly, stirring occasionally. Reduce heat to low; cover and cook 6 to 8 minutes or until apples are tender, stirring occasionally.

2. In small bowl, combine flour, sugar and salt; stir into apple mixture. Cook until mixture thickens, stirring constantly. Remove from heat; stir in vanilla and margarine. Cool 15 to 20 minutes.

3. Meanwhile, heat oven to 375°F. Prepare pastry for *one-crust pie* as directed. On floured surface, roll out dough to 11-inch round. Place on ungreased cookie sheet.

4. Spoon fruit mixture evenly onto half of pastry to within ½ inch of edge. In small bowl, beat 1 tablespoon water and egg; brush over edges of pastry. Fold remaining side of pastry over fruit, turnover fashion; press edges firmly to seal. Flute edge; cut small slits in top. Brush top with egg mixture.

5. Bake at 375°F. for 25 to 35 minutes or until crust is golden brown. Serve warm or cool.

Yield: 4 servings

Country Lemon Tart with Butter Pecan Crust

The butter pecan, press-in crust complements the tart lemon flavor of the filling.

Prep Time: 15 minutes
(Ready in 1 hour 40 minutes)

CRUST

1¼ cups Martha White® All Purpose Flour
⅓ cup finely chopped pecans
3 tablespoons powdered sugar
¼ teaspoon salt
½ cup butter or margarine, softened
1 egg yolk

FILLING

3 eggs
1 cup sugar
1 tablespoon Martha White® All Purpose Flour
1½ teaspoons grated lemon peel
3 tablespoons lemon juice

Powdered sugar

1. Heat oven to 350°F. Lightly grease 9-inch pie pan. In large bowl, combine all crust ingredients; mix well with fork. Shape dough into ball. With floured hands, press dough evenly in bottom and up sides of greased pie pan. Bake at 350°F. for 10 minutes.

2. Meanwhile, in medium bowl, beat eggs. Add 1 cup sugar, flour, lemon peel and lemon juice; beat until smooth.

3. Remove partially baked crust from oven. Pour filling into crust. Return to oven; bake an additional 20 to 25 minutes or until filling is set. Cool on wire rack for 1 hour or until completely cooled. Before serving, lightly sprinkle pie with powdered sugar. Store in refrigerator.

Yield: 10 servings

Classic Cheesecake Tart with Chocolate Pecan Crust

Prep Time: 15 minutes
(Ready in 1 hour 45 minutes)

CRUST

1 cup powdered sugar
½ cup butter or margarine, softened
1 egg yolk
1 cup Martha White® All Purpose Flour
2 tablespoons unsweetened cocoa
½ teaspoon baking powder
1 cup ground pecans*

FILLING

3 (8-oz.) pkg. cream cheese, softened
1 cup sugar
1½ teaspoons vanilla
4 eggs

1. Heat oven to 350°F. Grease and flour 13x9-inch pan. In large bowl, combine powdered sugar, butter and egg yolk; beat with electric mixer until well blended.

2. Add flour, cocoa and baking powder; mix well. Stir in pecans. Press in bottom of greased and floured pan.

3. In another large bowl, combine cream cheese, sugar and vanilla; beat with electric mixer until light and fluffy. Add eggs 1 at a time, beating well after each addition. Spoon and spread mixture over crust in pan.

4. Bake at 350°F. for 30 minutes or until filling is set and light brown around edges. Cool on wire rack for 1 hour or until completely cooled. Refrigerate until well chilled before serving. Store in refrigerator.

Yield: 18 servings

TIP: * Pecans can be ground in food processor or blender.

Country Lemon Tart with Butter Pecan Crust

Cumberland Apple Tart with Oat Crust

Prep Time: 20 minutes
(Ready in 1 hour 45 minutes)

CRUST
½   cup butter or margarine, softened
¼   cup firmly packed brown sugar
1   cup Martha White® All Purpose Flour
½   cup finely chopped pecans, if desired
¼   cup quick-cooking rolled oats

FILLING
2   large Golden Delicious apples
    Juice of half lemon
½   cup sugar
½   teaspoon cinnamon

1. Heat oven to 375°F. Lightly grease 9-inch pie pan. In large bowl, combine butter and brown sugar; beat with electric mixer until well blended. Add flour, pecans and oats; blend well. Shape dough into ball. With floured hands, press dough evenly in bottom and up sides of greased pie pan.

2. Peel and slice apples to measure about 3 cups; toss with juice of half lemon. Arrange apple slices evenly in crust in circular pattern, starting from outside edge and working toward center. Fill in any spaces until all apple slices are used. In small bowl, combine sugar and cinnamon; mix well. Sprinkle evenly over apples.

3. Bake at 375°F. for 35 to 40 minutes or until crust is light golden brown and apples are tender. Cool on wire rack for at least 45 minutes before serving. Store in refrigerator.

Yield: 10 servings

Winter Cranberry Tart with Brown Sugar Crust

Prep Time: 15 minutes
(Ready in 1 hour 50 minutes)

CRUST
2½   cups Martha White® All Purpose Flour
⅓   cup firmly packed brown sugar
½   teaspoon salt
10   tablespoons butter or margarine

FILLING
3   eggs
⅔   cup firmly packed brown sugar
1   tablespoon cornstarch
½   teaspoon salt
⅔   cup light corn syrup
¼   cup butter or margarine, melted
1   teaspoon vanilla
1¼   cups (about 6 oz.) coarsely chopped cranberries
1   cup coarsely chopped walnuts

1. Heat oven to 350°F. Grease 13x9-inch pan. In medium bowl, combine flour, ⅓ cup brown sugar and ½ teaspoon salt; mix well. With pastry blender or fork, cut in 10 tablespoons butter until mixture is crumbly. Press mixture firmly in bottom and about 1 inch up sides of greased pan. Bake at 350°F. for 20 minutes.

2. Meanwhile, in large bowl, beat eggs. Add all remaining filling ingredients except cranberries and walnuts; mix until smooth. Stir in cranberries and walnuts.

3. Remove partially baked crust from oven. Pour filling into crust. Return to oven; bake an additional 25 minutes or until filling is set. Cool on wire rack for 1 hour or until completely cooled. Store in refrigerator.

Yield: 18 servings

Cumberland Apple Tart with Oat Crust

Old-Fashioned Peach Cobbler

This classic cobbler recipe features baked strips of pastry layered throughout the filling.

Prep Time: 30 minutes (Ready in 2 hours)

CRUST

4	**cups Martha White® All Purpose Flour**
1¼	**teaspoons salt**
1⅓	**cups shortening**
⅔	**cup water**

FILLING

2	**cups sugar**
3	**tablespoons Martha White® All Purpose Flour**
7	**cups sliced fresh or frozen peaches**
1	**cup water**
½	**teaspoon almond extract**
½	**cup butter or margarine, cut into small pieces**

1. Heat oven to 400°F. In large bowl, combine 4 cups flour and salt; mix well. With pastry blender or fork, cut in shortening until mixture resembles coarse crumbs. Add ⅔ cup water, 1 tablespoon at a time, tossing and mixing lightly with fork. Add water until dough is just moist enough to form a ball when lightly pressed together.

2. Shape dough into smooth ball. Divide dough into 3 pieces. On lightly floured surface, roll out 1 piece of dough as thin as possible, about ⅛ inch thick. With floured knife or pizza cutter, cut dough into 3x1-inch strips. Place strips on ungreased cookie sheet. Cover remaining 2 pieces of dough.

3. Bake at 400°F. for 8 minutes or until strips are lightly browned. Cool on wire rack. Reduce oven temperature to 375°F.

4. Meanwhile, grease 13x9-inch (3-quart) baking dish. In large bowl, combine sugar and 3 tablespoons flour; mix well. Add peaches, 1 cup water and almond extract; stir to blend. Roll out 1 piece of remaining dough in shape of baking dish to about ⅛-inch thickness. Fit pastry in bottom and up sides of greased baking dish, leaving 1-inch overhang.

5. Spoon half of filling into unbaked pastry shell. Top with half of butter. Scatter baked pastry strips over filling. Spoon remaining filling over pastry strips. Top with remaining butter.

6. Roll out remaining piece of dough in shape of baking dish to about ⅛-inch thickness. With floured knife or pizza cutter, cut into ¾-inch-wide strips. Weave strips of crust to form a lattice top over filling. Seal and flute edge as desired.

7. Bake at 375°F. for 50 to 60 minutes or until crust is golden brown and filling begins to bubble. Cool on wire rack for at least 30 minutes before serving.

Yield: 10 servings

Easy Fresh Peach Cobbler

Prep Time: 15 minutes (Ready in 1 hour)

BATTER
- ½ cup butter or margarine, melted
- 1½ cups Martha White® Self-Rising Flour
- ⅓ cup sugar
- 1¼ cups milk

FRUIT MIXTURE
- 5 cups sliced peeled peaches
- 1 cup sugar
- ⅛ teaspoon almond extract, if desired

1. Heat oven to 350°F. Pour melted butter into 13x9-inch (3-quart) baking dish, coating bottom evenly. Set aside.

2. In medium bowl, combine all remaining batter ingredients; mix well. Pour batter evenly over butter in baking dish.

3. In large bowl, combine all fruit mixture ingredients; toss to mix. Spoon evenly over batter. Do not stir.

4. Bake at 350°F. for 40 to 45 minutes or until golden brown and bubbly. Serve warm with ice cream or whipped cream, if desired.

Yield: 10 servings

Blueberry-Peach Cobbler

Prep Time: 15 minutes (Ready in 45 minutes)

- 2 (21-oz.) cans peach pie filling
- 1 (7-oz.) pkg. Martha White® Blueberry Muffin Mix
- ¾ cup milk
- ¼ cup butter or margarine, melted

1. Heat oven to 400°F. Grease 13x9-inch (3-quart) baking dish. Spoon pie filling into greased baking dish.

2. In bowl, combine all remaining ingredients; mix well. Pour evenly over pie filling.

3. Bake at 400°F. for 25 to 30 minutes or until golden brown.

Yield: 10 servings

Easy Summer Berry Cobbler

Prep Time: 15 minutes
(Ready in 1 hour 5 minutes)

BATTER
- ½ cup butter or margarine
- 1 cup Martha White® Self-Rising Flour
- ¼ cup sugar
- ¾ cup milk

FRUIT MIXTURE
- 1 cup fresh blueberries
- 1 cup fresh raspberries
- ½ cup sugar
- ½ cup water

1. Heat oven to 350°F. Place butter in 8-inch square (2-quart) baking dish or 2-quart casserole; place in oven to melt.

2. In medium bowl, combine flour, ¼ cup sugar and milk; blend well. Pour batter evenly over melted butter in baking dish.

3. In another medium bowl, combine all fruit mixture ingredients; mix gently. Spoon evenly over batter in baking dish. Do not stir.

4. Bake at 350°F. for 45 to 50 minutes or until golden brown and bubbly. Serve warm.

Yield: 6 servings

Mom's Apple Cobbler

Mom's Apple Cobbler

This autumn favorite is made cinnamon-roll style. The cranberry-apple variation is perfect for the holidays.

**Prep Time: 35 minutes
(Ready in 1 hour 20 minutes)**

- ½   **cup butter or margarine**
- 2   **cups sugar**
- 2   **cups water**
- 1½   **cups Martha White® Self-Rising Flour**
- ½   **cup shortening**
- ⅓   **cup milk**
- 2   **cups finely chopped peeled baking apples**
- 1   **teaspoon cinnamon**

1. Heat oven to 350°F. Place butter in 13x9-inch (3-quart) baking dish; place in oven to melt. In medium saucepan, combine sugar and water; heat over medium heat until sugar dissolves, stirring frequently. Set aside.

2. Place flour in medium bowl. With pastry blender or fork, cut in shortening until mixture resembles coarse crumbs. Add milk; stir with fork just until mixture begins to pull away from sides of bowl.

3. On lightly floured surface, knead dough just until smooth. Roll out dough to 12x10x¼-inch rectangle.

4. In medium bowl, combine apples and cinnamon; stir to mix. Sprinkle apples evenly over dough. Beginning with long side, roll up jelly-roll fashion. Cut into 16 slices, each about ½ inch thick. Arrange slices in baking dish over melted butter. Pour sugar syrup carefully around and over rolls. (This looks like too much liquid, but crust will absorb it.)

5. Bake at 350°F. for 40 to 45 minutes or until golden brown. Cool 15 minutes before serving.

Yield: 10 servings

CRANBERRY APPLE COBBLER: Use 1 cup chopped fresh cranberries and 1 cup finely chopped peeled apple.

APPLE RAISIN PECAN COBBLER: Sprinkle ½ cup raisins over melted butter in baking dish; arrange dough slices over raisins. Sprinkle top with ½ cup chopped pecans before baking.

Sweet Biscuit Cobbler

Prep Time: 10 minutes (Ready in 35 minutes)

- 1   **(21-oz.) can fruit pie filling**
- 1   **cup Martha White® Self-Rising Flour**
- ¼   **cup sugar**
- ¼   **cup milk**
- 3   **tablespoons butter or margarine, melted**

1. Heat oven to 400°F. Lightly grease 8-inch square (2-quart) baking dish. Pour pie filling into greased baking dish; spread evenly.

2. In medium bowl, combine flour and sugar; mix well. Add milk and butter; stir just until blended. Drop dough by spoonfuls onto pie filling, making about 9 biscuits.

3. Bake at 400°F. for 22 to 25 minutes or until biscuits are golden brown. Serve warm or cool.

Yield: 6 servings

Winter Dried Apple Cobbler

Strips of buttery biscuit dough top a dried-apple filling.

**Prep Time: 20 minutes
(Ready in 1 hour 10 minutes)**

COBBLER
- 3 cups water
- 1½ cups sugar
- ¼ cup lemon juice
- 1⅔ cups Martha White® Self-Rising Flour
- ½ cup butter or margarine
- ½ cup milk
- 2 (6-oz.) pkg. dried apples, coarsely chopped

TOPPING
- 1 tablespoon milk
- 2 tablespoons sugar

1. Heat oven to 350°F. Grease 13x9-inch (3-quart) baking dish. In medium saucepan, combine water and 1½ cups sugar; heat over medium heat until sugar dissolves, stirring frequently. Remove from heat; add lemon juice. Set aside.

2. Place flour in large bowl. With pastry blender or fork, cut in butter until mixture resembles coarse crumbs. Add ½ cup milk; stir with fork just until mixture pulls away from sides of bowl.

3. On floured surface, knead dough just until smooth. Roll out dough to 12-inch square. Cut dough into 8 strips. Place 3 strips lengthwise in bottom of greased baking dish. Sprinkle apples evenly over dough. Place remaining strips of dough lengthwise over apples.

4. Pour sugar syrup carefully between strips of dough. Brush dough with 1 tablespoon milk; sprinkle with 2 tablespoons sugar.

5. Bake at 350°F. for 40 to 50 minutes or until golden brown. Serve warm or cool.

Yield: 12 servings

Stir and Bake Fruit Cobbler

Prep Time: 10 minutes (Ready in 40 minutes)
- 1 (21-oz.) can fruit pie filling
- ¾ cup Martha White® Self-Rising Flour
- ⅓ cup sugar
- ¾ cup milk
- ⅓ cup butter or margarine, melted
- 1 teaspoon vanilla

1. Heat oven to 400°F. Lightly grease 8-inch square (2-quart) baking dish. Pour pie filling into greased baking dish; spread evenly.

2. In medium bowl, combine flour and sugar; mix well. Add remaining ingredients; stir just until smooth. Pour batter over pie filling in baking dish.

3. Bake at 400°F. for 25 to 30 minutes or until golden brown. Serve warm or cool.

Yield: 6 servings

Cherry Crunch

Prep Time: 10 minutes (Ready in 40 minutes)
- 1 (21-oz.) can cherry pie filling
- ¾ cup Martha White® Self-Rising Flour
- ¾ cup firmly packed brown sugar
- ⅓ cup butter or margarine
- ½ cup chopped pecans

1. Heat oven to 375°F. Lightly grease 8-inch square (2-quart) baking dish. Pour pie filling into greased baking dish; spread evenly.

2. In bowl, combine flour and brown sugar; mix well. With pastry blender or fork, cut in butter until crumbly. Stir in pecans. Sprinkle mixture over pie filling in baking dish.

3. Bake at 375°F. for 25 to 30 minutes or until topping is deep golden brown. Serve warm or cool.

Yield: 6 servings

Winter Dried Apple Cobbler

Superfast Blueberry Cobbler

Prep Time: 10 minutes (Ready in 1 hour)

- ½ cup butter or margarine, melted
- 1 cup Martha White® Self-Rising Flour
- ¾ cup sugar
- ¾ cup milk
- 2 cups fresh or frozen blueberries
- ½ cup water

1. Heat oven to 350°F. Pour melted butter in 10x6-inch (1½-quart) baking dish, coating bottom evenly. In medium bowl, combine flour, ¼ cup of the sugar and the milk; blend well. Pour evenly over butter in baking dish.

2. In large bowl, combine blueberries, remaining ½ cup sugar and water; spoon evenly over batter in baking dish. Do not stir.

3. Bake at 350°F. for 45 to 50 minutes or until golden brown and bubbly.

Yield: 6 servings

Apple Pecan Crisp

It's great with apples, but you'll want to use this crisp topping on any fruit in season.

Prep Time: 15 minutes (Ready in 50 minutes)

FRUIT MIXTURE
- ¾ cup sugar
- 2 tablespoons Martha White® Self-Rising Flour
- ½ teaspoon cinnamon
- 6 cups sliced peeled Golden Delicious apples

TOPPING
- 1 cup Martha White® Self-Rising Flour
- 1 cup firmly packed brown sugar
- 10 tablespoons butter or margarine
- 1 cup rolled oats
- ½ cup chopped pecans

1. Heat oven to 350°F. Grease 13x9-inch (3-quart) baking dish. In large bowl, combine sugar, 2 tablespoons flour and cinnamon; mix well. Add apples; stir to coat evenly. Pour into greased baking dish.

2. In medium bowl, combine 1 cup flour and brown sugar; mix well. With pastry blender or fork, cut in butter until mixture resembles coarse crumbs. Stir in oats and pecans. Sprinkle crumb mixture evenly over fruit mixture.

3. Bake at 350°F. for 30 to 35 minutes or until topping is golden brown.

Yield: 8 servings

TIP: If desired, 2 (21-oz.) cans apple pie filling can be substituted for the fruit mixture.

Cobbler Classifications

There are five basic types of cobbler. Each is different, delicious and just fine for enhancing seasonal fresh fruits.

CLASSIC: Fruit with strips of raw or pre-baked pie crust layered in the fruit mixture and baked on top.

BISCUIT: Fruit topped with rich biscuit dough, either dropped, rolled out in strips or cut with a biscuit cutter, then baked.

POUR-BATTER: Fruit topped with a buttery liquid batter that bakes into a tender cakey topping.

CRISP: Fruit sprinkled with a crumbly mixture of flour and butter (often with nuts or oatmeal) and baked up buttery and crisp.

BAKE-THROUGH: With this dessert, the batter goes in the bottom of the baking dish and the fruit on top. As if by magic, the batter bakes up through the fruit, producing a golden brown crust.

Apple Pecan Crisp

Cookies
& Brownies

The first baking experience for many kids is making a batch of cookies. Little do they know that getting elbow deep in cookie dough is a shrewd tactic, used by many a parent or grandparent, for teaching basic kitchen skills. There's nothing like the sense of accomplishment that accompanies enjoying a cold glass of milk and a warm cookie you've made yourself.

Carmelicious Turtle Brownies, page 172

Buttery Sugar Cookies

Prep Time: 1 hour 30 minutes
(Ready in 2 hours 30 minutes)

1	**cup sugar**
1	**cup butter or margarine, softened**
1	**teaspoon vanilla**
2	**eggs**
3	**cups Martha White® All Purpose Flour**

1. In large bowl, combine sugar and butter; beat with electric mixer until light and fluffy. Add vanilla and eggs; blend well. Add flour; mix well. Cover with plastic wrap; refrigerate at least 1 hour for easier handling.

2. Heat oven to 350°F. On lightly floured surface, roll dough to 1/8-inch thickness. Cut with 2 1/2-inch round or shaped cutter. Place 1 inch apart on ungreased cookie sheets.

3. Bake at 350°F. for 10 to 12 minutes or until light golden brown. Cool 1 minute; remove from cookie sheets. Cool 10 minutes or until completely cooled. Decorate as desired.

Yield: 6 dozen cookies

Party Pecan Balls

Prep Time: 1 hour 15 minutes
(Ready in 2 hours 15 minutes)

1 1/4	**cups powdered sugar**
1/2	**cup butter or margarine, softened**
1	**teaspoon vanilla**
1	**cup Martha White® All Purpose Flour**
1/8	**teaspoon salt**
1	**cup finely chopped pecans**

1. In medium bowl, combine 1/4 cup of the powdered sugar and the butter; beat with electric mixer until light and fluffy. Add vanilla; blend well. Add flour and salt; mix well. Stir in pecans. Cover with plastic wrap; refrigerate at least 1 hour for easier handling.

2. Heat oven to 350°F. Grease cookie sheets. Shape dough into 1/2-inch balls. Place 1 inch apart on greased cookie sheets.

3. Bake at 350°F. for 12 to 15 minutes or until light golden brown. Immediately remove from cookie sheets. Place remaining 1 cup powdered sugar in shallow bowl. Roll each warm cookie in sugar. Cool 15 minutes or until completely cooled.

Yield: 5 dozen cookies

Country Lemon Squares

Prep Time: 30 minutes
(Ready in 1 hour 15 minutes)

CRUST
- 2 cups Martha White® All Purpose Flour
- ¼ cup sugar
- ½ teaspoon salt
- ½ cup butter or margarine, melted
- ½ cup finely chopped pecans

FILLING
- 2 cups sugar
- 2 tablespoons Martha White® All Purpose Flour
- 1 tablespoon grated lemon peel, if desired
- 6 tablespoons lemon juice
- 6 eggs, beaten

Powdered sugar

1. Heat oven to 350°F. Grease 13x9-inch pan. In medium bowl, combine 2 cups flour, ¼ cup sugar, salt and butter; mix until crumbly. Stir in pecans. Press mixture in bottom of greased pan. Bake at 350°F. for 20 minutes or until light golden brown.

2. In another medium bowl, combine 2 cups sugar, 2 tablespoons flour, lemon peel, lemon juice and eggs; beat until smooth.

3. Pour filling over partially baked crust. Return to oven; bake an additional 20 to 25 minutes or until filling is set. Cool 30 minutes or until completely cooled. Sprinkle with powdered sugar. Cut into squares.

Yield: 18 servings

Pecan Pie Squares

Prep Time: 30 minutes (Ready in 2 hours)

CRUST
- 2 cups Martha White® All Purpose Flour
- ¼ cup sugar
- ½ teaspoon salt
- ½ cup butter or margarine, melted

FILLING
- 2 cups chopped pecans
- 1 cup sugar
- 1 cup light corn syrup
- 2 tablespoons butter or margarine, melted
- 1 teaspoon vanilla
- 3 eggs, slightly beaten

1. Heat oven to 350°F. Grease 13x9-inch pan. In large bowl, combine all crust ingredients; mix until crumbly. Press mixture in bottom of greased pan. Bake at 350°F. for 20 minutes or until very light golden brown.

2. In medium bowl, combine all filling ingredients; mix well. Pour filling over partially baked crust; bake an additional 25 to 28 minutes or until filling is set. Cool 1 hour or until completely cooled. Cut into bars. Store in refrigerator.

Yield: 24 bars

Cookie Gems

Prep Time: 45 minutes

- ¾ cup sugar
- ½ cup butter or margarine
- 1 teaspoon vanilla
- 1 egg
- 2¾ cups Martha White® All Purpose Flour
- ½ teaspoon salt
- ¼ teaspoon baking powder
- ¼ teaspoon baking soda
- ½ cup sour cream
- 1¼ cups finely chopped nuts
  Any flavor jam, jelly or preserves

1. Heat oven to 400°F. Grease cookie sheets. In large bowl, combine sugar, butter, vanilla and egg; blend well.

2. In medium bowl, combine flour, salt, baking powder and baking soda; mix well. Add to butter mixture alternately with sour cream; mix well. Shape dough into 1¼-inch balls; roll in nuts.* Place 1 inch apart on greased cookie sheets. With thumb or end of wooden spoon, make indentation in center of each cookie. Spoon about ½ teaspoon jam into each indentation.

3. Bake at 400°F. for 10 to 12 minutes or until light golden brown.

Yield: 3½ dozen cookies

TIP: * If dough is sticky, add additional flour, 1 tablespoon at a time, until of desired consistency.

Coconut Pecan Triangles

Prep Time: 40 minutes

COOKIES
- 2 cups Martha White® All Purpose Flour
- ¼ cup sugar
- ½ teaspoon salt
- ¾ cup butter or margarine, melted

TOPPING
- 1½ cups firmly packed brown sugar
- 2 tablespoons Martha White® All Purpose Flour
- 1 teaspoon vanilla
- 2 eggs, slightly beaten
- 1 cup chopped pecans
- ½ cup coconut

1. Heat oven to 350°F. In medium bowl, combine all cookie ingredients; mix until crumbly. Press mixture in bottom of ungreased 13x9-inch pan. Bake at 350°F. for 20 minutes.

2. Meanwhile, in another medium bowl, combine brown sugar, 2 tablespoons flour, vanilla and eggs; beat until smooth. Add pecans and coconut; mix well.

3. Carefully spoon and spread pecan mixture over partially baked crust. Return to oven; bake an additional 15 to 17 minutes or until light golden brown. Cool 30 minutes or until completely cooled. Cut into triangle-shaped bars.

Yield: 36 bars

Cookie Gems

The Best Orange Date Bars

These thin, chewy bars have a great fresh orange flavor.

Prep Time: 20 minutes
(Ready in 1 hour 20 minutes)

BARS
- ¾ cup butter or margarine
- 1¼ cups Martha White® All Purpose Flour
- ¾ cup sugar
- 2 teaspoons grated orange peel
- ½ teaspoon baking powder
- ¼ teaspoon salt
- 1 egg
- 1 cup coarsely chopped pecans
- 1 (8-oz.) pkg. chopped dates

FROSTING
- 1 cup powdered sugar
- 1 (3-oz.) pkg. cream cheese, softened
- 1 teaspoon grated orange peel

1. Heat oven to 325°F. Grease 13x9-inch pan. Melt butter in large saucepan over low heat. Remove from heat. Add flour, sugar, 2 teaspoons orange peel, baking powder, salt and egg; blend well. Add pecans and dates; mix well. Spread batter in greased pan.

2. Bake at 325°F. for 25 to 30 minutes or until light golden brown and bars begin to pull away from sides of pan. Cool 30 minutes or until completely cooled.

3. In medium bowl, combine all frosting ingredients; blend until smooth. Spread frosting over cooled bars. Let stand until frosting is set. Cut into bars. Store in refrigerator.

Yield: 36 bars

Cherry Cheese Bars

Prep Time: 30 minutes
(Ready in 1 hour 10 minutes)

- ¾ cup sugar
- ¾ cup butter or margarine, softened
- 2 eggs
- 1½ cups plus 2 to 4 tablespoons Martha White® All Purpose Flour
- ¼ teaspoon salt
- 1 (8-oz.) pkg. cream cheese, softened
- 1 cup cherry preserves

1. Heat oven to 350°F. Grease 13x9-inch pan. In large bowl, combine sugar and butter; beat with electric mixer until light and fluffy. Add 1 of the eggs; beat well.

2. Add 1½ cups of the flour and the salt; blend well. Reserve 1 cup of mixture. With floured fingers, press remaining mixture in bottom of greased pan. Bake at 350°F. for 15 minutes.

3. Add remaining 2 to 4 tablespoons flour to reserved butter mixture; mix until crumbly. In small bowl, combine cream cheese and remaining egg; beat until smooth.

4. Spread cream cheese mixture evenly over partially baked crust. Carefully spoon and spread cherry preserves over cream cheese mixture. Sprinkle with reserved crumb mixture. Return to oven; bake an additional 35 to 40 minutes or until edges are golden brown. Cool 1 hour or until completely cooled. Cut into bars. Store in refrigerator.

Yield: 36 bars

Cherry Cheese Bars and The Best Orange Date Bars

Louisiana Praline Bars

Buttery, pecan praline flavor is wrapped up in this chewy one-pan bar cookie.

**Prep Time: 20 minutes
(Ready in 1 hour 55 minutes)**

BARS
- ¾ **cup butter or margarine**
- 1½ **cups firmly packed brown sugar**
- 2 **teaspoons vanilla**
- 2 **eggs**
- 2 **cups Martha White® Self-Rising Flour**
- ¼ **cup milk**
- 1 **cup chopped pecans**

GLAZE
- 2 **tablespoons butter or margarine**
- ¼ **cup firmly packed brown sugar**
- 2 **tablespoons milk**

1. Heat oven to 350°F. Grease bottom only of 13x9-inch pan. Melt ¾ cup butter in large saucepan over medium heat. Remove from heat.

2. Add brown sugar, vanilla and eggs; blend well. Add flour and milk; mix well. Spread batter in greased pan; sprinkle with pecans.

3. Bake at 375°F. for 30 to 35 minutes or until top is deep golden brown. Cool 1 hour or until completely cooled.

4. Melt 2 tablespoons butter in small saucepan over medium heat. Stir in remaining glaze ingredients. Bring to a boil. Cook 2 to 3 minutes or until slightly thickened, stirring constantly. Drizzle glaze over cooled bars. Let stand until glaze is set. Cut into bars.

Yield: 36 bars

Sour Cream Banana Bars

Freeze your overripe bananas, and you can whip up a batch of these bars anytime.

**Prep Time: 20 minutes
(Ready in 1 hour 15 minutes)**

BARS
- ½ **cup butter or margarine**
- 2 **cups Martha White® Self-Rising Flour**
- 1½ **cups sugar**
- 1½ **cups mashed ripe bananas**
  (about 3 medium)
- 1 **cup sour cream**
- 2 **teaspoons vanilla**
- 2 **eggs**

GLAZE
- 2 **cups powdered sugar**
- ¼ **cup butter or margarine, melted**
- 3 **tablespoons milk**

1. Heat oven to 350°F. Grease bottom only of 15x10x1-inch baking pan. Melt ½ cup butter in large saucepan over low heat. Remove from heat. Stir in all remaining bar ingredients; mix well. Spread batter in greased pan.

2. Bake at 350°F. for 20 to 25 minutes or until golden brown. Cool 30 minutes or until completely cooled.

3. In medium bowl, combine all glaze ingredients; blend until smooth. Drizzle glaze over cooled bars. Let stand until glaze is set. Cut into bars.

Yield: 60 bars

Smoky Mountain Jam Squares

This one-pan bar cookie boasts all the flavor of a classic jam cake.

Prep Time: 25 minutes (Ready in 2 hours)

BARS

¾ cup butter or margarine
1 cup firmly packed brown sugar
½ cup blackberry or strawberry jam
2 eggs
1 teaspoon vanilla
2 cups Martha White® Self-Rising Flour
½ teaspoon cinnamon
½ teaspoon cloves
1 cup chopped walnuts

GLAZE

2 tablespoons butter or margarine
¼ cup firmly packed brown sugar
3 tablespoons milk
1 cup powdered sugar
1 teaspoon vanilla

1. Heat oven to 350°F. Grease bottom only of 13x9-inch pan. Melt ¾ cup butter in large saucepan over medium heat. Remove from heat. Stir in all remaining bar ingredients in order listed, mixing well after each addition. Spread batter in greased pan.

2. Bake at 350°F. for 30 to 35 minutes or until top is golden brown. Cool 1 hour or until completely cooled.

3. Melt 2 tablespoons butter in small saucepan over medium heat. Stir in ¼ cup brown sugar and milk. Bring to a boil. Cook 1 minute, stirring constantly. Remove from heat. Stir in powdered sugar and 1 teaspoon vanilla. Drizzle glaze over cooled bars. Let stand until glaze is set. Cut into bars.

Yield: 36 bars

Shortbread Fruit Bars

Prep Time: 15 minutes
(Ready in 1 hour 15 minutes)

SHORTBREAD

2 cups Martha White® All Purpose Flour
½ cup sugar
1 cup butter
¾ cup blackberry or raspberry preserves

GLAZE

½ cup powdered sugar
½ teaspoon almond extract
2 to 3 teaspoons water

1. Heat oven to 350°F. In large bowl, combine flour and sugar; mix well. With pastry blender or fork, cut in butter until mixture resembles coarse crumbs. Press mixture in bottom of ungreased 13x9-inch pan.

2. Bake at 350°F. for 25 to 35 minutes or until edges are light golden brown.

3. Spread preserves over shortbread; bake an additional 5 minutes. Cool 1 hour or until completely cooled.

4. In small bowl, combine all glaze ingredients; mix well. Drizzle over cooled shortbread. Cut into bars.

Yield: 36 bars

Coco Not Cookies

This recipe was a specialty of Alice Jarman, the first director of the Martha White Kitchens. Instant potato flakes and coconut flavoring make these crisp little wafers taste authentic.

Prep Time: 1 hour

1	cup sugar
⅓	cup butter or margarine, softened
1	teaspoon coconut extract
1	egg
1	cup instant potato flakes
1	(5.5-oz.) pkg. Martha White® Buttermilk Biscuit Mix

1. Heat oven to 375°F. In large bowl, combine sugar and butter; beat until light and fluffy. Add coconut extract and egg; blend well.

2. Add potato flakes and biscuit mix; mix well. Shape dough into ¾-inch balls. Place 2 inches apart on ungreased cookie sheet.

3. Bake at 375°F. for 12 to 14 minutes or until golden brown. Remove from cookie sheet.

Yield: 4 dozen cookies

Fabulous Scotchies

There are enough variations to meet many occasions with this Martha White saucepan bar.

Prep Time: 15 minutes
(Ready in 1 hour 15 minutes)

1¼	cups Martha White® All Purpose Flour
½	teaspoon baking powder
¼	teaspoon salt
½	cup butter or margarine
1¼	cups firmly packed brown sugar
1	cup chopped pecans
1	teaspoon vanilla
2	eggs

1. Heat oven to 350°F. Grease 13x9-inch pan. In medium bowl, combine flour, baking powder and salt; mix well.

2. Melt butter in large saucepan over low heat. Remove from heat. Add flour mixture, brown sugar, pecans, vanilla and eggs; mix well. Spread batter in greased pan.

3. Bake at 350°F. for 25 to 30 minutes or until golden brown and bars begin to pull away from sides of pan. Cool 30 minutes or until completely cooled. Cut into bars.

Yield: 24 bars

FABULOUS CASHEW SCOTCHIES: Omit pecans. Top with 1 cup cashew pieces before baking.

FABULOUS CHOCOLATE CHIP SCOTCHIES: Stir 1 cup semi-sweet chocolate chips into batter.

Fabulous Scotchies

Lemon Butter Pound Cake Bars

A classic buttery pound cake takes on a lemon-fresh flavor in this easy bar cookie.

Prep Time: 15 minutes (Ready in 2 hours)

BARS

1	**cup butter or margarine**
2	**cups sugar**
4	**eggs**
2	**cups Martha White® Self-Rising Flour**
2	**tablespoons grated lemon peel**
⅓	**cup lemon juice**

GLAZE

1	**cup powdered sugar**
2	**tablespoons lemon juice**

1. Heat oven to 375°F. Grease bottom only of 13x9-inch pan. Melt butter in large saucepan over medium heat. Remove from heat. Stir in all remaining bar ingredients in order listed, mixing well after each addition. Spread batter in greased pan.

2. Bake at 375°F. for 35 to 45 minutes or until top is golden brown. Cool 10 minutes.

3. In small bowl, combine glaze ingredients; blend until smooth. Drizzle over bars. Cool 1 hour or until completely cooled. Cut into bars.

Yield: 48 bars

Ginger Geometrics

Press this gingerbread dough into a 15x10x1-inch (jelly-roll) pan, bake, cut into shapes and decorate. You'll be amazed at the time-saving shortcut.

Prep Time: 45 minutes

1	**cup sugar**
⅔	**cup oil**
¼	**cup molasses**
1	**egg**
2	**cups Martha White® All Purpose Flour**
2	**teaspoons baking soda**
1	**teaspoon cinnamon**
1	**teaspoon ginger**
½	**teaspoon salt**

1. Heat oven to 350°F. In large bowl, combine sugar, oil, molasses and egg; blend well. Add all remaining ingredients; mix well. Press dough evenly in ungreased 15x10x1-inch baking pan.

2. Bake at 350°F. for 15 minutes or until set. DO NOT OVERBAKE. Cool 15 minutes or until completely cooled. Cut into desired shapes.

Yield: 5 dozen cookies

Bar Cookie Celebration

Great bar cookie recipes are easy solutions to enjoying homemade sweets without spending hours in the kitchen. Bar cookies taste just as great as traditional cookies, and they offer the added convenience of one-time, one-pan baking. Cutting bar cookies into different shapes instantly changes their character. A platter of triangles, diamonds, rectangles and squares looks fancy and irresistible.

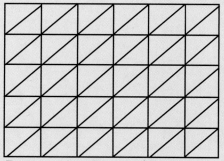

Diagram for Ginger Geometrics

Lemon Butter Pound Cake Bars

Caramelicious Turtle Brownies

Prep Time: 25 minutes (Ready in 2 hours)

BROWNIES

1	(22.5-oz.) pkg. Martha White® Chewy Fudge Brownie Mix
½	cup oil
½	cup water
1	egg

TOPPING

20	vanilla caramels, unwrapped
3	tablespoons milk
½	cup semi-sweet chocolate chips
½	cup chopped pecans or walnuts

1. Heat oven to 350°F. Grease bottom only of 13x9-inch pan. In large bowl, combine all brownie ingredients; beat 50 strokes with spoon. Spread batter in greased pan.

2. Bake at 350°F. for 27 to 30 minutes. DO NOT OVERBAKE.

3. Meanwhile, in small saucepan over medium-low heat, melt caramels with milk, stirring occasionally until smooth. Keep warm.

4. Sprinkle warm brownies with chocolate chips and pecans. Drizzle with hot caramel mixture. Cool 1 hour or until completely cooled. Cut into bars.

Yield: 24 bars

Peanut Butter Fudge Snack Bars

In about an hour's time, you can be enjoying one of life's best taste combinations—peanut butter and chocolate—with a tall glass of cold milk.

Prep Time: 15 minutes (Ready in 50 minutes)

BARS

½	cup butter or margarine
4	oz. unsweetened chocolate
2	cups sugar
½	cup water
3	eggs
1	teaspoon vanilla
1¾	cups Martha White® Self-Rising Flour

TOPPING

½	cup peanut butter
½	cup chopped salted peanuts

1. Heat oven to 350°F. Grease bottom only of 13x9-inch pan. In large saucepan, melt butter and chocolate over medium-low heat, stirring occasionally. Remove from heat.

2. Stir in all remaining bar ingredients in order listed, mixing well after each addition. Pour batter into greased pan.

3. Melt peanut butter in small saucepan over low heat, stirring occasionally. Drop peanut butter by small spoonfuls over batter. With knife, gently swirl peanut butter into batter to create marbled effect. Sprinkle with peanuts.

4. Bake at 350°F. for 30 to 35 minutes or until bars begin to pull away from sides of pan.

Yield: 24 servings

TIP: Peanut butter can be melted in small microwave-safe bowl in microwave oven.

Peanut Butter Fudge Snack Bars

Frosted Cashew Brownies

Prep Time: 20 minutes
(Ready in 1 hour 55 minutes)

BROWNIES

1	(22.5-oz.) pkg. Martha White® Chewy Fudge Brownie Mix
½	cup oil
½	cup water
1	egg
½	cup coarsely chopped cashews

FROSTING

¼	cup butter or margarine
¼	cup unsweetened cocoa
1½	cups powdered sugar
1	teaspoon vanilla
2	to 3 tablespoons milk
½	cup cashew halves

1. Heat oven to 350°F. Grease 13x9-inch pan. In large bowl, combine brownie mix, oil, water and egg; beat 50 strokes with spoon. Stir in chopped cashews. Spread batter in greased pan.

2. Bake at 350°F. for 27 to 30 minutes. DO NOT OVERBAKE. Cool 1 hour or until completely cooled.

3. Melt butter in medium saucepan over medium heat. Stir in cocoa. Bring just to a boil, stirring constantly. Cool slightly. Stir in powdered sugar, vanilla and enough milk for desired spreading consistency; blend until smooth. Spread frosting over cooled brownies. Sprinkle with cashew halves. Cool 1 hour or until completely cooled. Cut into bars.

Yield: 36 bars

Tuxedo Brownies

Prep Time: 40 minutes
(Ready in 1 hour 40 minutes)

BROWNIES

1	(12-oz.) pkg. Martha White® Chewy Fudge Brownie Mix
3	tablespoons oil
3	tablespoons water
1	egg

TOPPING

½	cup sugar
1	tablespoon Martha White® All Purpose Flour
1	(8-oz.) pkg. cream cheese, softened
2	tablespoons butter or margarine
1	teaspoon vanilla
2	eggs

1. Heat oven to 350°F. Grease bottom only of 9-inch square pan. In medium bowl, combine all brownie ingredients; beat 50 strokes with spoon. Spread batter in greased pan. Bake at 350°F. for 20 minutes.

2. Meanwhile, in another medium bowl, combine all topping ingredients; beat until smooth.

3. Spread cream cheese topping over partially baked brownies. Return to oven; bake an additional 20 minutes or until edges are golden brown and brownies begin to pull away from sides of pan. Cut into squares while warm. Cool 15 minutes. Refrigerate 30 minutes or until chilled. Store in refrigerator.

Yield: 16 bars

Mocha Buttercream Bars

Prep Time: 25 minutes (Ready in 2 hours)

BARS

1   (22.5-oz.) pkg. Martha White® Chewy
     Fudge Brownie Mix
½   teaspoon cinnamon
½   cup oil
½   cup water
1   egg

FROSTING

2   teaspoons instant coffee granules
     or crystals
4   teaspoons hot water
2   cups powdered sugar
2   tablespoons unsweetened cocoa
½   cup butter or margarine, softened

1. Heat oven to 350°F. Grease bottom only of 13x9-inch pan. In large bowl, combine all bar ingredients; beat 50 strokes with spoon. Spread batter in greased pan.

2. Bake at 350°F. for 27 to 30 minutes. DO NOT OVERBAKE. Cool 1 hour or until completely cooled.

3. In large bowl, dissolve coffee granules in hot water. Add all remaining frosting ingredients; beat until smooth. Spread frosting over cooled bars. Refrigerate at least 1 hour or until frosting is set. Cut into bars.

Yield: 36 bars

Brownie Dress-Ups

Start with a brownie mix and end up with your own signature dessert.

1. Sprinkle the batter with nuts or stir some in: almonds, walnuts, peanuts, macadamias and cashews taste great in brownies.

2. Check out the baking aisle for brownie fix-ups from peanut butter chips to miniature marshmallows to white chocolate chunks to English toffee bits. Serious chocolate lovers may opt for an extra handful of chocolate chips stirred into the batter.

3. Add an easy flavoring to the batter such as instant coffee powder, ground cinnamon or peppermint or almond extract.

4. Don't forget glazes and icings. Make your own or rely on prepared varieties from the grocery store.

Carmelicious Brownies, page 172

Peanut Crisp Brownies

Prep Time: 30 minutes
(Ready in 1 hour 25 minutes)

BROWNIES

1	**(22.5-oz.) pkg. Martha White® Chewy Fudge Brownie Mix**
½	**cup oil**
½	**cup water**
1	**egg**

TOPPING

2	**cups miniature marshmallows**
⅔	**cup light corn syrup**
¼	**cup butter or margarine**
2	**teaspoons vanilla**
1	**(10-oz.) pkg. peanut butter chips**
2	**cups crisp rice cereal**
1	**cup coarsely chopped salted peanuts**

1. Heat oven to 350°F. Grease bottom only of 13x9-inch pan. In large bowl, combine all brownie ingredients; beat 50 strokes with spoon. Spread batter in greased pan.

2. Bake at 350°F. for 27 to 30 minutes. DO NOT OVERBAKE. Remove from oven. Immediately sprinkle evenly with marshmallows. Return to oven; bake an additional 1 to 2 minutes or until marshmallows just begin to puff. Cool while preparing topping.

3. In large saucepan, combine corn syrup, butter, vanilla and chips. Cook over low heat just until mixture is melted and smooth, stirring constantly. Remove from heat. Stir in cereal and nuts. Immediately spoon and spread warm topping over marshmallows. Refrigerate until set. Cut into bars.

Yield: 36 bars

Saucepan Brownies

This Martha White Kitchens recipe has been around as long as anyone can remember, and it tastes just as great today as ever.

Prep Time: 15 minutes
(Ready in 1 hour 15 minutes)

½	**cup butter or margarine**
2	**oz. unsweetened chocolate**
1	**cup sugar**
2	**eggs**
¾	**cup Martha White® Self-Rising Flour**
1	**teaspoon vanilla**
¾	**cup chopped pecans**

1. Heat oven to 350°F. Grease 9-inch square pan. In medium saucepan, melt butter and chocolate over low heat until smooth, stirring constantly.

2. Add all remaining ingredients in order listed; mix well after each addition. Spread batter in greased pan.

3. Bake at 350°F. for 25 to 30 minutes or until brownies begin to pull away from sides of pan. Cool 30 minutes or until completely cooled. Cut into bars.

Yield: 16 bars

Creamy Strawberry Brownie Delight

Prep Time: 20 minutes (Ready in 2 hours)

BROWNIES
- 1 (22.5-oz.) pkg. Martha White® Chewy Fudge Brownie Mix
- ½ cup water
- ½ cup oil
- 1 egg

TOPPING
- 2 (8-oz.) pkg. cream cheese
- 1 (16-oz.) can vanilla frosting
- 3 cups sliced fresh strawberries

1. Heat oven to 350°F. Grease bottom only of 13x9-inch pan. In large bowl, combine brownie mix, water, oil and egg; beat 50 strokes with spoon. Spread in greased pan.

2. Bake at 350°F. for 27 to 30 minutes. DO NOT OVERBAKE. Cool 1 hour or until completely cooled.

3. In a small bowl, combine cream cheese and frosting; beat until smooth. Spread evenly over cooled brownies. Arrange strawberry slices over cream cheese mixture. Refrigerate until serving time. Store in refrigerator.

Yield: 16 bars

TIP: If desired, melt ¼ cup chocolate chips with ½ teaspoon oil; cool slightly. Drizzle over strawberry slices.

Rocky Road Fudge Brownies

Prep Time: 20 minutes (Ready in 2 hours)

BROWNIES
- 1 (22.5-oz.) pkg. Martha White® Chewy Fudge Brownie Mix
- ½ cup water
- ½ cup oil
- 1 egg

TOPPING
- 2 cups miniature marshmallows
- 1 cup salted peanuts
- ½ cup caramel topping

1. Heat oven to 350°F. Grease bottom only of 13x9-inch pan. In large bowl, combine brownie mix, water, oil and egg; beat 50 strokes with spoon. Spread in greased pan.

2. Bake at 350°F. for 27 to 30 minutes. DO NOT OVERBAKE. Remove pan from oven. Immediately sprinkle with marshmallows and peanuts. Drizzle with caramel topping.

3. Return to oven. Bake an additional 5 to 7 minutes or until marshmallows begin to puff. Cool 1 hour or until completely cooled. (For ease in cutting, use non-serrated knife dipped in water.)

Yield: 20 bars

Walnut Ganache Brownies

Your guests will think you've spent hours on these brownies topped with ganache, an icing made with cream and chocolate.

Prep Time: 30 minutes
Ready in 1 hour 30 minutes

BROWNIES
- 2 (12-oz.) pkg. Martha White® Chewy Fudge Brownie Mix
- 1 cup butter, melted, cooled
- ¼ cup water
- 1 teaspoon vanilla
- 2 eggs, beaten
- 1 cup coarsely chopped walnuts

GANACHE
- ¼ cup whipping cream
- 1 (6-oz.) pkg. (1 cup) semi-sweet chocolate chips

1. Heat oven to 350°F. Grease bottom only of 13x9-inch pan. In large bowl, combine brownie mixes, butter, water, vanilla and eggs; beat 50 strokes with spoon. Stir in walnuts. Spread batter in greased pan.

2. Bake at 350°F. for 27 to 29 minutes. Cool 30 minutes or until completely cooled. Store in refrigerator.

3. In medium saucepan, bring whipping cream to a boil. Remove from heat. Add chocolate chips; stir until melted and smooth. Spread over cooled brownies. Cut into bars. Store in refrigerator.

Yield: 24 bars

White Chocolate Chunk Brownies

Prep Time: 15 minutes
(Ready in 1 hour 15 minutes)

- 2 (12-oz.) pkg. Martha White® Chewy Fudge Brownie Mix
- 6 tablespoons oil
- ¼ cup water
- 2 eggs
- 6 oz. white chocolate baking bar, coarsely chopped
- 1 cup coarsely chopped walnuts
- ¾ cup semi-sweet chocolate chips

1. Heat oven to 350°F. Grease bottom only of 13x9-inch pan. In large bowl, combine brownie mixes, oil, water and eggs; beat 50 strokes with spoon. Fold in baking bar and walnuts. Spread batter in greased pan. Bake at 350°F. for 26 to 28 minutes.

2. Remove pan from oven. Immediately sprinkle evenly with chocolate chips. Return to oven; bake an additional 1 minute or until chips are melted. Spread chips evenly over brownies. Cool 30 minutes or until completely cooled. Cut into 24 squares. Cut each square in half to form triangles.

Yield: 48 bars

White Chocolate Chunk Brownies

Cakes

Carry in a pristine fresh coconut cake, velvety pound cake or even an everyday applesauce cake, and watch as all eyes are drawn to your creation. Immediately, the tone is set for celebration. In fact, all good traditional Southern cakes tend to have active social lives—the honor of their presence is requested at occasions year after year. It must be because a homemade cake means someone spent a generous amount of time and effort in the kitchen, all in the name of pleasing others.

Fresh Coconut Cake, Page 182

Fresh Coconut Cake

This quintessential Southern favorite is made a bit easier to prepare with marshmallow frosting.

**Prep Time: I hour
(Ready in 2 hours 35 minutes)**

CAKE
2½ cups Martha White® All Purpose Flour
3½ teaspoons baking powder
I teaspoon salt
I½ cups sugar
I cup milk
¾ cup shortening
I½ teaspoons vanilla
5 egg whites
I fresh coconut, drained, reserving milk, peeled and grated (3 cups)

FROSTING
½ cup sugar
2 tablespoons water
2 egg whites
I (7-oz.) jar (I½ cups) marshmallow creme
I teaspoon vanilla

I. Heat oven to 350°F. Grease and flour two 9-inch round cake pans or two 8-inch square pans. In medium bowl, combine flour, baking powder and salt; mix well. Add 1½ cups sugar, ¾ cup of the milk, shortening and 1½ teaspoons vanilla; blend well. Beat at low speed 30 seconds. Beat at medium speed 2 minutes.

2. Add remaining ¼ cup milk and 5 egg whites. Beat at high speed 2 minutes. Pour batter into greased and floured pans.

3. Bake at 350°F. for 30 to 35 minutes or until cake begins to pull away from sides of pan and toothpick inserted in center comes out clean. Cool 10 minutes. Remove from pans. Cool 1 hour or until completely cooled. Make several holes in surface of layers with toothpick; pour reserved coconut milk over layers.

4. In medium saucepan, combine ½ cup sugar, water and 2 egg whites. Cook over low heat, beating continuously with electric hand mixer at high speed until soft peaks form.

5. Add marshmallow creme; beat until stiff peaks form. Remove saucepan from heat. Beat in 1 teaspoon vanilla.

6. To assemble cake, place 1 layer, top side down, on serving plate. Spread with frosting. Top with remaining layer, top side up; spread sides and top of cake with frosting. Sprinkle sides and top of cake generously with grated coconut.

Yield: 16 servings

Brown Sugar Pound Cake

Prep Time: 30 minutes
(Ready in 2 hours 45 minutes)

CAKE

2¼	cups firmly packed brown sugar
½	cup sugar
1	cup butter or margarine, softened
½	cup shortening
2	teaspoons vanilla
5	eggs
3	cups Martha White® All Purpose Flour
½	teaspoon baking powder
¼	teaspoon salt
1	cup milk
1	cup chopped pecans

GLAZE

¼	cup butter or margarine
½	cup firmly packed brown sugar
¼	cup milk
1	teaspoon vanilla
2	cups powdered sugar

1. Heat oven to 350°F. Grease and flour 10-inch tube pan. In large bowl, combine 2¼ cups brown sugar, sugar, 1 cup butter, shortening and 2 teaspoons vanilla; beat until light and fluffy. Add eggs 1 at a time, beating well after each addition.

2. In medium bowl, combine flour, baking powder and salt; mix well. Add flour mixture to butter mixture alternately with milk, beating well after each addition. Stir in pecans. Spread batter in greased and floured pan.

3. Bake at 350°F. for 1¼ hours or until toothpick inserted in center comes out clean. Cool 10 minutes. Remove from pan. Cool 1 hour or until completely cooled.

4. Melt ¼ cup butter in small saucepan over medium-low heat. Add ½ cup brown sugar; cook 2 minutes, stirring constantly. Add ¼ cup milk; bring to a boil, stirring constantly.

5. Remove saucepan from heat. Stir in vanilla. Gradually stir in powdered sugar; blend until smooth. Drizzle over cooled cake.

Yield: 16 servings

Buttermilk Chess Pound Cake

Buttermilk Chess Pound Cake

Made with flour and self-rising corn meal mix, this recipe is a delicious example of how a little corn meal can transform a classic recipe. Try it lightly buttered and toasted for breakfast.

Prep Time: 20 minutes
(Ready in 2 hours 55 minutes)

- 2½ cups sugar
- 1 cup butter or margarine, softened
- 1 teaspoon vanilla
- 5 eggs
- 2 cups Martha White® All Purpose Flour
- 1 cup Martha White® Self-Rising Corn Meal Mix
- 1 cup buttermilk

1. Heat oven to 350°F. Grease and flour 10-inch tube or 12-cup Bundt® pan. In large bowl, combine sugar, butter and vanilla; beat until light and fluffy. Add eggs 1 at a time, beating well after each addition.

2. In medium bowl, combine flour and corn meal mix. Add to butter mixture alternately with buttermilk, beginning and ending with flour. Mix well after each addition. Pour batter into greased and floured pan.

3. Bake at 350°F. for 50 to 65 minutes or until toothpick inserted in center comes out clean. Cool 30 minutes. Remove from pan. Cool 1 hour or until completely cooled.

Yield: 16 servings

Bundt® is a registered trademark of Northland Aluminum Products, Inc., Minneapolis, MN.

Poppy Seed Orange Cake

Prep Time: 30 minutes
(Ready in 2 hours 30 minutes)

- 4 egg whites
- 1⅔ cups Martha White® All Purpose Flour
- ¾ cup sugar
- 1 tablespoon poppy seed
- 2 teaspoons baking powder
- ¼ teaspoon salt
- ½ cup oil
- ½ cup orange juice
- 2 teaspoons grated orange peel

1. Heat oven to 350°F. Spray bottom of 8x4-inch loaf pan with nonstick cooking spray. In small bowl, beat egg whites at high speed until stiff peaks form.

2. In large bowl, combine flour, sugar, poppy seed, baking powder and salt; mix well. Add oil and orange juice; beat at medium speed until smooth. (Batter will be thick.) Add orange peel and about ⅓ of the egg whites; stir gently. Fold in remaining egg whites. Pour batter into sprayed pan.

3. Bake at 350°F. for 45 minutes or until toothpick inserted in center comes out clean. Cool in pan 10 minutes. Remove from pan. Cool 1 hour or until completely cooled.

Yield: 12 servings

Walnut Raisin Pound Cake

Easy Chocolate Sheet Cake

Just about as popular as brownies, this cake is a classic in recipe files across the South.

Prep Time: 30 minutes
(Ready in 1 hour 50 minutes)

CAKE

½	cup buttermilk*
1	teaspoon baking soda
¼	cup unsweetened cocoa
1	cup water
½	cup butter or margarine
½	cup oil or melted shortening
1	teaspoon vanilla
2	eggs, slightly beaten
2	cups Martha White® All Purpose Flour
2	cups sugar
1	teaspoon cinnamon

FROSTING

¼	cup unsweetened cocoa
½	cup butter or margarine
¼	cup milk
1	teaspoon vanilla
4	cups powdered sugar

1. Heat oven to 400°F. Grease and flour 13x9-inch pan. In small bowl, combine buttermilk and baking soda; mix well.

2. In medium saucepan, combine ¼ cup cocoa, water, ½ cup butter and oil. Bring to a boil over medium heat, stirring constantly.

3. Remove from heat; stir in buttermilk mixture and 1 teaspoon vanilla. Add eggs; blend well. Add flour, sugar and cinnamon; mix well. Pour batter into greased and floured pan.

4. Bake at 400°F. for 15 to 20 minutes or until toothpick inserted in center comes out clean. Cool 1 hour or until completely cooled.

5. In medium saucepan, combine ¼ cup cocoa, ½ cup butter and milk. Bring to a boil over medium heat, stirring constantly. Remove saucepan from heat. Stir in 1 teaspoon vanilla. Gradually stir in powdered sugar; blend until smooth. Spread frosting over top of cooled cake.

Yield: 15 servings

TIP: * To substitute for buttermilk, use 1½ teaspoons vinegar or lemon juice plus milk to make ½ cup.

Walnut Raisin Pound Cake

Prep Time: 30 minutes
(Ready in 2 hours 40 minutes)

1¾	cups sugar
1	cup butter or margarine, softened
1	teaspoon vanilla
4	eggs
2¼	cups Martha White® All Purpose Flour
¼	teaspoon salt
¼	teaspoon nutmeg
2	cups golden raisins or chopped dates
2	cups coarsely chopped walnuts

1. Heat oven to 325°F. Grease and flour 10-inch tube pan. In large bowl, combine sugar and butter; beat until light and fluffy. Add vanilla; blend well. Add eggs 1 at a time, beating well after each addition.

2. Add 2 cups of the flour, salt and nutmeg; mix well. In small bowl, combine raisins and remaining ¼ cup flour; toss to coat. Add coated raisins and walnuts; mix well. Spoon batter into greased and floured pan.

3. Bake at 325°F. for 1 hour 10 minutes or until toothpick inserted in center comes out clean. Cool in pan 10 minutes. Remove from pan. Cool 1 hour or until completely cooled.

Yield: 16 servings

Chocolate Sour Cream Pound Cake

Chocolate Sour Cream Pound Cake

Cut this loaf cake into three horizontal layers and fill it with vanilla, almond or mocha filling.

Prep Time: 30 minutes
(Ready in 2 hours 50 minutes)

CAKE
1½	**cups sugar**
½	**cup butter or margarine, softened**
1	**teaspoon vanilla**
4	**eggs**
1½	**cups Martha White® All Purpose Flour**
¼	**teaspoon baking soda**
⅛	**teaspoon salt**
1	**cup sour cream**
3	**oz. unsweetened chocolate, melted, cooled**
	Powdered sugar

VANILLA FILLING
¼	**cup butter or margarine, softened**
1	**(8-oz.) pkg. cream cheese, softened**
1	**teaspoon vanilla**
¾	**cup powdered sugar**

1. Heat oven to 325°F. Grease and flour 9x5-inch loaf pan. In large bowl, combine 1½ cups sugar and ½ cup butter; beat until light and fluffy. Add 1 teaspoon vanilla; blend well. Add eggs 1 at a time, beating well after each addition.

2. In large bowl, combine flour, baking soda and salt; mix well. Add to butter mixture alternately with sour cream, beginning and ending with flour mixture. Add melted chocolate; blend well. Pour batter into greased and floured pan.

3. Bake at 325°F. for 1 hour 20 minutes or until toothpick inserted in center comes out clean. Cool 10 minutes. Remove from pan. Cool 1 hour or until completely cooled.

4. In small bowl, combine ¼ cup butter and cream cheese; beat until light and fluffy. Add 1 teaspoon vanilla. Gradually beat in ¾ cup powdered sugar.

5. To assemble cake, split cake horizontally to make 3 layers. Place 1 layer on serving plate. Spread with ½ of filling; repeat with second layer and remaining filling. Top with remaining layer; sprinkle with additional powdered sugar. Store in refrigerator.

Yield: 12 servings

ALMOND FILLING: Prepare vanilla filling as directed, substituting ½ teaspoon almond extract for the 1 teaspoon vanilla.

MOCHA FILLING: Prepare vanilla filling as directed, omitting vanilla. Increase powdered sugar to 1 cup. Dissolve ¼ teaspoon instant coffee granules in 1 tablespoon water; beat into cream cheese mixture with 1 tablespoon unsweetened cocoa.

Sour Cream Pound Cake

This is a recipe that the Martha White Kitchens staff absolutely cannot live without.

**Prep Time: 15 minutes
(Ready in 2 hours 35 minutes)**

2¾	cups sugar
1½	cups butter, softened
1	teaspoon vanilla
6	eggs
3	cups Martha White® All Purpose Flour
1	teaspoon grated orange or lemon peel
½	teaspoon baking powder
½	teaspoon salt
1	cup sour cream

1. Heat oven to 350°F. Generously grease and flour 12-cup Bundt® pan. In large bowl, combine sugar and butter; beat until light and fluffy. Add vanilla; blend well. Add eggs 1 at a time, beating well after each addition.

2. In medium bowl, combine flour, orange peel, baking powder and salt. Add flour mixture to butter mixture alternately with sour cream, beating well after each addition. Pour batter into greased and floured pan.

3. Bake at 350°F. for 55 to 65 minutes or until toothpick inserted in center comes out clean. Cool 15 minutes. Invert cake onto serving plate. Cool 1 hour or until completely cooled.

Yield: 16 servings

Kentucky Butter Cake

**Prep Time: 30 minutes
(Ready in 1 hour 40 minutes)**

CAKE

3	cups Martha White® All Purpose Flour
2	cups sugar
1	teaspoon salt
1	teaspoon baking powder
½	teaspoon baking soda
1	cup buttermilk*
1	cup butter, softened
2	teaspoons vanilla or rum extract
4	eggs

BUTTER SAUCE

¾	cup sugar
⅓	cup butter
3	tablespoons water
1	to 2 teaspoons vanilla or rum extract

GARNISH

2	to 3 teaspoons powdered sugar

1. Heat oven to 325°F. Generously grease and lightly flour 12-cup Bundt® or 10-inch tube pan. In large bowl, combine all cake ingredients; beat at low speed until moistened. Beat 3 minutes at medium speed. Pour batter into greased and floured pan.

2. Bake at 325°F. for 55 to 70 minutes or until toothpick inserted in center comes out clean.

3. In small saucepan, combine all butter sauce ingredients; cook over low heat until butter melts, stirring occasionally. DO NOT BOIL. With long-tined fork, pierce cake 10 to 12 times. Slowly pour hot sauce over warm cake. Let stand 5 to 10 minutes or until sauce is absorbed.

4. Invert cake onto serving plate. Just before serving, sprinkle with powdered sugar. Serve with whipped cream, if desired.

Yield: 16 servings

TIP: * To substitute for buttermilk, use 1 tablespoon vinegar or lemon juice plus milk to make 1 cup.

Old-Fashioned Jam Cake

This version of the spicy holiday cake is flavored with both blackberry jam and strawberry preserves. The brown sugar glaze is an updated version of the classic caramel icing.

Prep Time: 45 minutes
(Ready in 2 hours 35 minutes)

CAKE
1	cup sugar
½	cup butter or margarine
½	teaspoon vanilla
3	eggs
1½	cups Martha White® All Purpose Flour
½	teaspoon baking soda
½	teaspoon allspice
½	teaspoon cinnamon
½	teaspoon cloves
¼	teaspoon salt
½	cup buttermilk*
1	cup blackberry jam
½	cup strawberry preserves
½	cup raisins
½	cup chopped walnuts

GLAZE
¼	cup butter or margarine
½	cup firmly packed dark brown sugar
¼	cup milk
1	teaspoon vanilla
2	cups powdered sugar

1. Heat oven to 325°F. Grease bottoms only of two 8-inch square or round cake pans. Line pans with waxed paper; grease and flour paper and sides of pans. In large bowl, combine sugar and ½ cup butter; beat until light and fluffy.

2. Add ½ teaspoon vanilla; blend well. Add eggs 1 at a time, beating well after each addition. Add flour, baking soda, allspice, cinnamon, cloves, salt, buttermilk, jam and preserves. Beat 2 minutes at medium speed. Stir in raisins and walnuts. Pour batter into greased and floured pans.

3. Bake at 325°F. for 45 to 50 minutes or until toothpick inserted in center comes out clean. Cool 10 minutes. Remove from pans. Cool 1 hour or until completely cooled.

4. Melt ¼ cup butter in medium saucepan over medium-low heat. Stir in brown sugar; cook 2 minutes, stirring constantly. Add milk; bring to a boil, stirring constantly. Remove from heat. Stir in 1 teaspoon vanilla. Gradually stir in powdered sugar; blend until smooth.

5. To assemble cake, place 1 layer on serving plate. Spoon and spread about ⅓ of warm glaze over layer. Top with remaining layer. Spoon and spread remaining glaze over cake. Store in refrigerator.

Yield: 15 servings

TIP: * To substitute for buttermilk, use 1½ teaspoons vinegar or lemon juice plus milk to make ½ cup.

Applesauce Cake with Hot-Milk Icing

Applesauce Cake with Hot-Milk Icing

Nothing says "down home" quite like an applesauce cake, and the hot-milk icing ensures an extra-moist texture.

Prep Time: 30 minutes
(Ready in 1 hour 25 minutes)

CAKE
- 1¾ cups sugar
- ¼ cup firmly packed brown sugar
- ½ cup butter or margarine
- 2 eggs
- 2½ cups Martha White® Self-Rising Flour
- 1 teaspoon cinnamon
- ½ teaspoon nutmeg
- ¼ teaspoon allspice
- 1⅔ cups applesauce
- ⅔ cup raisins, if desired
- ½ cup chopped nuts, if desired

ICING
- ¼ cup milk
- 2 cups powdered sugar
- 2 tablespoons butter or margarine, melted
- ½ teaspoon vanilla

1. Heat oven to 325°F. Grease and flour 13x9-inch pan. In large bowl, combine sugar, brown sugar and ½ cup butter; beat until light and fluffy. Add eggs 1 at a time, beating well after each addition.

2. In medium bowl, combine flour, cinnamon, nutmeg and allspice; mix well. Add flour mixture to butter mixture alternately with applesauce, beating well after each addition. Stir in raisins and nuts. Spread batter in greased and floured pan.

3. Bake at 325°F. for 50 to 55 minutes or until cake pulls away from sides of pan. Cool slightly.

4. Heat milk in medium saucepan over low heat just until warm. Remove from heat. Add all remaining icing ingredients; beat until smooth. Spoon and spread over warm cake.

Yield: 18 servings

Spicy Carrot Cake

Prep Time: 20 minutes
(Ready in 1 hour 25 minutes)

- 1¼ cups Martha White® Self-Rising Flour
- 1 cup sugar
- 2 teaspoons cinnamon
- ¾ cup oil
- 2 teaspoons vanilla
- 2 eggs
- 1 cup grated carrots
- ½ to 1 cup chopped pecans
- ½ cup raisins
- Powdered sugar

1. Heat oven to 350°F. Grease bottom only of 8- or 9-inch square pan. In large bowl, combine flour, sugar, cinnamon, oil, vanilla and eggs; beat at low speed until moistened. Beat 2 minutes at medium speed. Stir in carrots, pecans and raisins. Pour into greased pan.

2. Bake at 350°F. for 50 to 65 minutes or until toothpick inserted in center comes out clean. Sprinkle with powdered sugar.

Yield: 9 servings

German Chocolate Surprise Cake

German Chocolate Surprise Cake

The is an easy upside-down version of German Chocolate Cake.

Prep Time: 25 minutes
(Ready in 1 hour 10 minutes)

TOPPING
- 1 cup chopped pecans
- ½ cup firmly packed brown sugar
- ½ cup flaked coconut
- ¼ cup butter or margarine, melted

CAKE
- ¼ cup water
- 2 oz. sweet baking chocolate
- 1 cup sugar
- ½ cup butter or margarine, softened
- 1 teaspoon vanilla
- 2 eggs
- 1¼ cups Martha White® Self-Rising Flour
- ½ cup milk

1. Heat oven to 350°F. In ungreased 9-inch round cake pan, combine all topping ingredients; mix well. Spread evenly in pan.

2. In small microwave-safe bowl, combine ¼ cup water and chocolate. Microwave on HIGH for 1 to 1½ minutes or until chocolate is melted. Stir to blend.

3. In medium bowl, combine sugar and ½ cup butter; beat until light and fluffy. Add vanilla and eggs; blend well. Add ¾ cup of the flour and the milk; mix well. Add remaining ½ cup flour; mix well. Stir in chocolate mixture. Pour batter over topping in pan.

4. Bake at 350°F. for 40 to 45 minutes or until toothpick inserted in center comes out clean. Loosen edge of cake with knife. Invert onto serving plate.

Yield: 8 servings

Lemon-Orange Picnic Cake

Prep Time: 15 minutes
(Ready in 1 hour 35 minutes)

CAKE
- 1 cup Martha White® All Purpose Flour
- ¾ cup sugar
- 1½ teaspoons grated orange peel
- 1 teaspoon grated lemon peel
- 1 teaspoon baking powder
- ¼ teaspoon salt
- ⅓ cup milk
- ¼ cup shortening
- 2 tablespoons orange juice
- 3 egg whites

TOPPING
- ¼ cup sugar
- 2 teaspoons lemon juice
- 1 teaspoon orange juice

1. Heat oven to 350°F. Spray bottom only of 8-inch square pan with nonstick cooking spray. In large bowl, combine all cake ingredients; beat at low speed until moistened. Beat 2 minutes at medium speed. Pour into sprayed pan.

2. Bake at 350°F. for 25 to 32 minutes or until cake is light golden brown and toothpick inserted in center comes out clean.

3. In small bowl, combine all topping ingredients; mix well. Spread over warm cake. Cool 45 minutes or until completely cooled.

Yield: 9 servings

Easy Butter Cake with Tart Lemon Filling

Prep Time: 35 minutes
(Ready in 2 hours 30 minutes)

CAKE

2	cups Martha White® All Purpose Flour
2	teaspoons baking powder
¾	teaspoon salt
1¼	cups sugar
⅔	cup butter, softened
⅔	cup milk
1	teaspoon vanilla
3	eggs

FILLING

¾	cup sugar
¼	cup cornstarch
1	cup water
2	egg yolks, slightly beaten
2	tablespoons butter
1	tablespoon grated lemon peel
¼	cup lemon juice

FROSTING

3	cups powdered sugar, sifted
½	cup butter, softened
3	tablespoons milk
2	teaspoons vanilla

1. Heat oven to 350°F. Grease and flour two 9-inch round cake pans. In large bowl, combine flour, baking powder and salt; mix well. Add all remaining cake ingredients. Beat at low speed for 30 seconds. Beat 3 minutes at high speed. Pour batter into greased and floured pans.

2. Bake at 350°F. for 20 to 25 minutes or until toothpick inserted in center comes out clean. Cool 10 minutes. Remove from pans. Cool 1 hour or until completely cooled.

3. In medium saucepan, combine sugar and cornstarch; gradually stir in water. Cook over medium heat until mixture boils and thickens, stirring constantly. Boil 1 minute. Gradually stir about ½ cup of hot mixture into egg yolks. Return egg mixture to saucepan. Bring to a boil. Cook 1 to 2 minutes, stirring constantly. Remove from heat. Add 2 tablespoons butter, lemon peel and lemon juice; stir until smooth. Cool 30 minutes or until completely cooled.

4. In large bowl, combine all frosting ingredients; beat until smooth.

5. To assemble cake, place 1 layer on serving plate. Spread filling within ¾ inch of edge. Top with remaining cake layer. Frost sides and top of cake with frosting.

Yield: 16 servings

SIMPLY CINNAMON CAKE: For cake, add 2 teaspoons cinnamon to dry ingredients, decrease sugar to ¾ cup and add ¾ cup firmly packed brown sugar. For frosting, add 1 teaspoon cinnamon. To assemble, spread frosting between layers, on top and on sides of cake. Sprinkle with ¼ cup finely chopped pecans; if desired, drizzle with chocolate syrup.

Top to bottom: Easy Butter Cake with Tart Lemon Filling; Simply Cinnamon Cake

Shortcakes

Desserts & Party Snacks

In the South, there is always a reason to celebrate, and food seems to be the focal point of the festivities. Any occasion qualifies for good eating. It can be a family reunion, holiday open house, bridal tea, Sunday dinner, fish fry, autumn tailgate picnic, Derby day—even the arrival of the first summer peaches. With no shortage of reasons to celebrate, maybe the best reason is no reason at all.

Easy Sour Cream Drop Shortcake, page 205

Apricot Cream Cheese Shortcake

Apricot Cream Cheese Shortcake

Prep Time: 1 hour
(Ready in 1 hour 30 minutes)

SHORTCAKE

    **Easy Rich Biscuit Shortcake
(made with Almond Drop Biscuit
variation)**

FILLING

    2   **cups water**
    1   **(6-oz.) pkg. dried apricots, cut into
bite-sized pieces**
    ½   **cup sugar**
    2   **tablespoons butter or margarine**
    ½   **teaspoon vanilla**

TOPPING

    2   **(3-oz.) pkg. cream cheese, softened**
    2   **tablespoons sugar**
    6   **tablespoons whipping cream**

1. Prepare and bake shortcakes as directed
in recipe. Cool.

2. Meanwhile, in medium saucepan, combine
water and apricots. Bring to a boil. Reduce
heat; cover and cook about 15 minutes or until
apricots are tender. Stir in ½ cup sugar and
butter. Simmer 30 to 40 minutes or until
thickened, stirring frequently. Cool 30 minutes
or until completely cooled. Stir in vanilla.

3. In small bowl, combine all topping
ingredients; beat until smooth and creamy.
Split shortcakes. Fill and top with apricot
mixture and cream cheese topping. Store
in refrigerator.

Yield: 10 shortcakes

Easy Rich Biscuit Shortcake

Prep Time: 25 minutes

    2   **cups Martha White® Self-Rising Flour**
    3   **tablespoons sugar**
    ⅓   **cup butter or margarine**
    1   **egg**
    ⅓   **to ½ cup milk**

1. Heat oven to 450°F. Grease cookie sheet. In
medium bowl, combine flour and sugar; mix
well. With pastry blender or fork, cut in butter
until mixture resembles coarse crumbs.

2. In 1-cup measuring cup, beat egg; add
enough milk to make ⅔ cup. Add to flour
mixture; stir with fork just until blended.

3. On lightly floured surface, knead dough
just until smooth. Roll out dough to about
½-inch thickness. Cut with floured 2½-inch
cutter into desired shapes. Place on greased
cookie sheet.

4. Bake at 450°F. for 10 to 12 minutes or until
golden brown. Serve warm.

Yield: 10 shortcakes

TIP: For drop biscuit shortcakes, add additional milk
until soft dough forms. Drop dough by spoonfuls onto
greased cookie sheet. Bake as directed above.

ALMOND DROP BISCUIT VARIATION: Add
additional milk until soft dough forms. Drop dough by
spoonfuls onto greased cookie sheet. Top with ¼ cup
sliced almonds. Bake as directed above.

Buttery Layered Shortcake

Prep Time: 25 minutes
(Ready in 1 hour 45 minutes)

2	cups Martha White® Self-Rising Flour
2	tablespoons sugar
¼	cup shortening
¾	cup milk
¼	cup butter or margarine, softened
6	cups sliced strawberries, sweetened to taste*
1	cup whipping cream
1	tablespoon sugar

1. Lightly grease large cookie sheet. In medium bowl, combine flour and 2 tablespoons sugar; mix well. With pastry blender or fork, cut in shortening until mixture resembles coarse crumbs. Add milk; stir just until dry ingredients are moistened.

2. On lightly floured surface, knead dough just until smooth. Roll out dough to 12x8-inch rectangle, about ⅓ inch thick. Spread butter evenly over dough. Fold dough crosswise into thirds by overlapping ends to form 3 layers and making 8x4-inch rectangle. Place on greased cookie sheet; cover with plastic wrap. Refrigerate 1 hour.

3. Heat oven to 425°F. Cut dough into 10 rectangles. Return dough to greased cookie sheet, placing rectangles 1 inch apart. Bake at 425°F. for 15 to 18 minutes or until golden brown. Serve warm or cool.

4. In small bowl, combine whipping cream and 1 tablespoon sugar; beat until soft peaks form. Split shortcakes. Fill and top with strawberries. Top each serving with whipped cream. Store in refrigerator.

Yield: 10 servings

TIP: * Raspberries, blackberries or sliced peeled peaches can be substituted for the strawberries.

Southern Biscuit Shortcake

Buttery, lightly sweetened biscuit, sweetened fresh berries and whipped cream make true Southern shortcake.

Prep Time: 20 minutes (Ready in 35 minutes)

2	cups Martha White® Self-Rising Flour
2	tablespoons sugar
⅓	cup butter or margarine
¾	cup half-and-half
6	cups sliced fresh fruit or berries, sweetened to taste
1	cup whipping cream
1	tablespoon sugar

1. Heat oven to 450°F. Lightly grease large cookie sheet. In medium bowl, combine flour and 2 tablespoons sugar; mix well. With pastry blender or fork, cut in butter until mixture resembles coarse crumbs. Add half-and-half; stir just until dry ingredients are moistened.

2. On lightly floured surface, knead dough just until smooth. Roll out dough to ½-inch thickness. Cut with floured cutter or knife into desired shapes. Place about 1 inch apart on greased cookie sheet.

3. Bake at 450°F. for 9 to 12 minutes or until golden brown. Serve warm or cool.

4. In small bowl, combine whipping cream and 1 tablespoon sugar; beat until soft peaks form. Split shortcakes. Fill and top with fruit. Top each serving with whipped cream. Store in refrigerator.

Yield: 10 servings

Southern Biscuit Shortcake

Cranberry Apple Shortcake

Prep Time: 25 minutes

SHORTCAKE
> **Easy Rich Biscuit Shortcake (page 201)**

FILLING AND TOPPING
- 2 tablespoons butter or margarine
- ½ cup firmly packed brown sugar
- ½ cup apple juice
- 4 medium Golden Delicious apples, peeled, sliced
- 1 cup fresh or frozen cranberries
  Whipped cream

1. Prepare and bake shortcakes as directed in recipe. Cool.

2. Meanwhile, melt butter in large skillet. Stir in brown sugar, apple juice, apples and cranberries; stir gently to mix. Simmer about 10 minutes or until apples are tender and liquid has thickened, stirring occasionally.

3. Split shortcakes. Fill and top with apple-cranberry mixture. Top each serving with whipped cream.

Yield: 10 servings

Pear Cranberry Shortcake

Prep Time: 50 minutes

SHORTCAKE
> **Easy Rich Biscuit Shortcake (page 201)**

FILLING AND TOPPING
- 2 tablespoons butter or margarine
- ½ cup sugar
- ¼ cup orange juice
- 4 medium pears, peeled, sliced
- 1 cup fresh or frozen cranberries
  Whipping cream

1. Prepare and bake shortcakes as directed in recipe. Cool.

2. Meanwhile, melt butter in large skillet over low heat. Stir in sugar, orange juice, pears and cranberries; stir gently to mix. Simmer 20 to 25 minutes or until pears are tender and liquid has thickened, stirring occasionally.

3. Split shortcakes. Fill and top with pear-cranberry mixture. Drizzle each serving with whipping cream.

Yield: 10 servings

Easy Sour Cream Drop Shortcake

This is the easiest homemade shortcake of all.

Prep Time: 25 minutes (Ready in 50 minutes)

- 2 **cups Martha White® Self-Rising Flour**
- 3 **tablespoons sugar**
- ⅔ **cup milk**
- ⅓ **cup sour cream**
- ¼ **cup butter or margarine, melted**
- 6 **cups sliced strawberries or peaches, sweetened to taste**
- I **cup whipping cream**
- I **tablespoon sugar**

I. Heat oven to 400°F. Lightly grease large cookie sheet. In medium bowl, combine flour and 3 tablespoons sugar; mix well. In small bowl, combine milk, sour cream and butter; blend well. Add to dry ingredients; stir just until dry ingredients are moistened. Drop dough by heaping large spoonfuls onto greased cookie sheet.

2. Bake at 400°F. for 20 to 25 minutes or until golden brown. Serve warm or cool.

3. In small bowl, combine whipping cream and 1 tablespoon sugar; beat until soft peaks form. Split shortcakes. Fill and top with strawberries or peaches. Top each serving with whipped cream. Store in refrigerator.

Yield: 10 servings

Banana Caramel Pecan Shortcake

Prep Time: 25 minutes

SHORTCAKE
> **Easy Rich Biscuit Shortcake (page 201)**

FILLING AND TOPPING
- ¼ **cup butter or margarine**
- ½ **cup pecan halves**
- ½ **cup firmly packed brown sugar**
- ½ **cup whipping cream**
- 4 **medium bananas, sliced**
- **Whipped cream**

I. Prepare and bake shortcakes as directed in recipe. Cool.

2. Meanwhile, melt butter in large skillet. Add pecans; cook over medium heat for about 2 minutes, stirring constantly. Add brown sugar and cream; cook and stir until well blended and sugar is dissolved. Stir in bananas; cook just until thoroughly heated.

3. Split shortcakes. Fill and top with banana mixture. Top each serving with whipped cream. Store in refrigerator.

Yield: 10 servings

Shortcake Sheetcake

With the addition of a single egg, biscuit dough becomes more cakelike, but it still holds up to fruit and juices.

Prep Time: 25 minutes (Ready in 1 hour)

- 2 **cups Martha White® Self-Rising Flour**
- ⅔ **cup sugar**
- ⅔ **cup butter or margarine**
- ⅔ **cup milk**
- 1 **egg, beaten**
- 6 **cups fresh berries, sweetened to taste**
- 1 **cup whipping cream**
- 1 **tablespoon sugar**

1. Heat oven to 375°F. Grease bottom only of 13x9-inch pan. In large bowl, combine flour and ⅔ cup sugar; mix well. With pastry blender or fork, cut in butter until mixture resembles coarse crumbs. Add milk and egg; stir just until dry ingredients are moistened. Spread batter evenly in greased pan.

2. Bake at 375°F. for 25 to 35 minutes or until golden brown. Serve warm or cool.

3. In small bowl, combine whipping cream and 1 tablespoon sugar; beat until soft peaks form. Cut shortcake into 12 squares. Split squares. Fill and top with berries. Top each serving with whipped cream. Store in refrigerator.

Yield: 12 servings

Sautéed Fruit with Shortcake Dumplings

Drop spoonfuls of dough on the hot fruit mixture and this dessert will be ready in 10 minutes.

Prep Time: 25 minutes

FRUIT MIXTURE
- ¾ **cup firmly packed brown sugar**
- ½ **cup orange juice**
- ¼ **cup butter or margarine**
- 8 **cups fresh or frozen sliced peeled peaches**
- 2 **cups fresh or frozen berries (such as blueberries, blackberries, raspberries and/or strawberries)**

DUMPLINGS
- 1½ **cups Martha White® Self-Rising Flour**
- 3 **tablespoons sugar**
- ½ **cup milk**
- 2 **tablespoons butter or margarine, melted**
- ½ **teaspoon vanilla**

TOPPING
- **Whipping cream, if desired**

1. In 12-inch skillet, combine brown sugar, orange juice and ¼ cup butter; mix well. Bring to a boil. Stir in peaches; return to a boil. Reduce heat to low; gently stir in berries. Simmer 5 minutes.

2. Meanwhile, in medium bowl, combine flour and sugar; mix well. Add milk, 2 tablespoons butter and vanilla; stir just until dry ingredients are moistened.

3. Drop dough by tablespoonfuls onto simmering fruit mixture. Cover; simmer 8 to 10 minutes or until dumplings are firm. Spoon into bowls; drizzle with whipping cream.

Yield: 8 servings

Desserts

Corn Meal on the Dessert Menu

Beyond a sprinkling in chess pie, corn meal has traditionally staked its claim to the savory side of the Southern menu. But, nowadays it seems down-home corn meal has become a chic addition to dessert menus nationwide. The Martha White Kitchens did a little experimenting and found that there is a secret to corn meal's sweet success. To enjoy its texture and flavor in desserts from mush custard to buttermilk chess pound cake, you have to pre-cook the corn meal a little or combine it with flour to lighten the texture.

Real Southern Shortcake is a Biscuit

Even in this age of convenience, there are still some things that shouldn't be compromised. Traditional shortcake, one of the South's greatest pleasures, definitely tops the list. Real shortcake is not a cake, but a buttery, lightly sweetened biscuit that can stand up to a soaking from juicy berries without turning into a soggy mess.

After mastering shortcake, take care with the fruit, too. Whether fresh strawberries, blackberries, raspberries or peaches, fruits are most flavorful when served at room temperature. Just before preparing the shortcake, toss the cut fruit with sugar to sweeten it and bring out the juices. By the time the shortcake is done, the sweetened fruit will be bathed in a juicy nectar. And don't scrimp on the whipped cream. Real whipped cream takes only minutes to prepare, and it's worth it.

Easy Sour Cream Drop Shortcake, page 205

Lemon Spoon Bread with Berries

A sweet version of a corn meal soufflé, this lemony pudding is at home at a casual barbecue or an elegant dinner.

Prep Time: 15 minutes (Ready in 55 minutes)

- 1 **cup Martha White® Self-Rising Corn Meal Mix**
- 1½ **cups milk**
- 3 **eggs, separated**
- ⅔ **cup sugar**
- 2 **teaspoons grated lemon peel**
- ⅓ **cup lemon juice**
- ¼ **cup butter or margarine**
- 2 **cups blackberries, raspberries and/or strawberries, sweetened to taste**

1. Heat oven to 375°F. Grease deep 2-quart casserole or 8-cup soufflé dish. Place corn meal mix in large bowl. In small saucepan, bring milk just to a boil. Gradually add milk to corn meal mix, stirring until smooth and thickened. Set aside.

2. In medium bowl, beat egg whites until soft peaks form. Set aside.

3. Add egg yolks, sugar, lemon peel, lemon juice and butter to corn meal mixture; beat well. Fold beaten egg whites into corn meal mixture. Pour into greased casserole.

4. Bake at 375°F. for 35 to 40 minutes or until golden brown and set. Serve warm. Top each serving with berries.

Yield: 8 servings

Old-Fashioned Biscuit Pudding

The Martha White version of bread pudding made with leftover biscuits.

Prep Time: 10 minutes (Ready in 40 minutes)

- 8 **Martha White Hot Rize® Biscuits (page 9)**
- ½ **cup firmly packed brown sugar**
- ½ **cup sugar**
- 2 **cups milk**
- ½ **cup butter or margarine, melted**
- 1 **teaspoon vanilla**
- 2 **eggs, beaten**
  Whipping cream, if desired

1. Prepare and bake biscuits as directed in recipe.

2. Heat oven to 425°F. Split 8 biscuits. In 10-inch cast iron skillet, place biscuit halves, split side up. Sprinkle brown sugar evenly over biscuits; sprinkle sugar over brown sugar.

3. In medium bowl, combine milk, butter, vanilla and eggs; beat well. Pour over biscuits.

4. Bake at 425°F. for 25 to 30 minutes or until golden brown. Serve warm. Drizzle each serving with whipping cream.

Yield: 8 servings

Lemon Spoon Bread with Berries

Banana Nut Muffin Pudding

Prep Time: 25 minutes
(Ready in 2 hours 25 minutes)

  1 **egg**
2⅓ **cups milk**
  1 **(7-oz.) pkg. Martha White® Banana Nut Muffin Mix**
  1 **(5.1-oz.) pkg. instant vanilla pudding and pie filling mix**
  1 **cup sour cream**
  2 **bananas, thinly sliced**

1. Heat oven to 400°F. Grease 6 muffin cups. In small bowl, beat egg. Add ⅓ cup of the milk and the muffin mix; stir just until blended. Fill muffin cups ⅔ full.

2. Bake at 400°F. for 13 to 15 minutes or until golden brown. Immediately remove from pan; cool on wire rack.

3. Meanwhile, in medium bowl, combine pudding mix, remaining 2 cups milk and sour cream. With wire whisk or electric mixer, beat 1 to 2 minutes or until well blended and thickened. Let stand 5 minutes or until soft-set.

4. Reserve half of 1 cooled muffin for garnish. Tear remaining muffins into bite-sized pieces. Place in bottom of ungreased 2-quart casserole or bowl. Arrange banana slices over muffins. Pour pudding over banana slices. Crumble reserved muffin half over pudding. Cover; refrigerate at least 2 hours or until serving time. If desired, garnish with additional banana slices.

Yield: 8 servings

Grits Cream

Lea Heil of Newberry, South Carolina, created this recipe and won the Grand Prize in the 1991 World Grits Festival Recipe Contest. The epitome of simple elegance, it shows plain grits can become a fancy dessert.

Prep Time: 15 minutes

½ **cup Jim Dandy® Quick Grits**
3 **tablespoons sugar**
¼ **teaspoon salt**
2½ **cups half-and-half**
1 **teaspoon vanilla**

1. In medium saucepan, combine grits, sugar, salt and half-and-half; mix well. Bring to a boil over medium heat. Cook about 8 minutes, stirring constantly.

2. Reduce heat; cook about 5 minutes or until thickened, stirring constantly. Stir in vanilla. Serve warm.

Yield: 6 servings

Grits Cream

Sautéed Peaches with Butter Pecan Dumplings

Prep Time: 30 minutes

FRUIT MIXTURE
- ¾ cup firmly packed brown sugar
- ½ cup orange juice
- ¼ cup butter or margarine
- 10 cups sliced peeled peaches

DUMPLINGS
- 1½ cups Martha White® Self-Rising Flour
- 3 tablespoons sugar
- ½ cup chopped pecans
- ½ cup milk
- 2 tablespoons butter or margarine, melted
- ½ teaspoon vanilla

1. In 12-inch skillet, combine brown sugar, orange juice and ¼ cup butter; mix well. Bring to a boil. Stir in peaches; return to a boil. Reduce heat to low; simmer 5 minutes.

2. Meanwhile, in medium bowl, combine flour and sugar; mix well. Add pecans, milk, 2 tablespoons butter and vanilla; stir just until dry ingredients are moistened.

3. Drop dough by tablespoonfuls onto simmering fruit mixture. Cover; simmer 8 to 10 minutes or until dumplings are firm.

Yield: 10 servings

Mush Custard with Dried Cherries

Corn meal mix is precooked in milk, then baked like a traditional egg custard for a rich cream taste and texture. The dried cherries add tartness and flair.

Prep Time: 20 minutes (Ready in 1 hour)

- 2½ cups milk
- ¾ cup Martha White® Self-Rising Corn Meal Mix
- ½ cup sugar
- 2 tablespoons butter or margarine
- 1 teaspoon vanilla
- ⅔ cup dried cherries or sweetened dried cranberries
- 4 eggs, beaten
- Whipped cream

1. Heat oven to 375°F. Grease 2-quart casserole. In large saucepan, bring 2 cups of the milk just to a boil. With wire whisk, gradually stir in corn meal mix. Cook, stirring constantly, until smooth and thickened. Remove from heat.

2. Add sugar, butter and vanilla; stir until butter is melted. Stir in remaining ½ cup milk and cherries. Add eggs; blend well. Pour mixture into greased casserole.

3. Bake at 375°F. for 35 to 40 minutes or until knife inserted near center comes out clean. Serve warm or cool. Top with whipped cream. Store in refrigerator.

Yield: 8 servings

Cheddar Cheese Sticks

Prep Time: 40 minutes
(Ready in 1 hour 40 minutes)

8	oz. (2 cups) shredded sharp Cheddar cheese
½	cup butter or margarine, softened
1½	cups Martha White® All Purpose Flour
½	teaspoon salt
⅛	teaspoon ground red pepper (cayenne)

1. In small bowl, combine cheese and butter; beat until blended. In medium bowl, combine flour, salt and ground red pepper; mix well. Add to cheese mixture; stir to blend or use hands to work in flour mixture. Cover dough; refrigerate 1 hour.

2. Heat oven to 375°F. Grease large cookie sheet. On lightly floured surface, knead dough gently just until smooth. Roll out dough until very thin, about 1/8-inch thickness. With sharp knife or pizza cutter, cut dough into 4x½-inch sticks. Place on greased cookie sheet.

3. Bake at 375°F. for 10 to 12 minutes or until golden brown. Cool at least 15 minutes on wire rack before serving.

Yield: 72 sticks

Easy Focaccia

Prep Time: 40 minutes

FOCACCIA

1	(6.5-oz.) pkg. Martha White® Pizza Crust Mix
½	cup hot water
1	teaspoon oil
	Melted butter or olive oil

TOPPING OPTIONS

Dried or fresh herbs, such as rosemary, thyme, basil, oregano or sage
Minced fresh garlic or garlic powder
Coarse salt
Coarse ground black pepper
Grated Parmesan cheese
Sesame seed

1. Place oven rack in lowest rack position in oven. Heat oven to 500°F. Grease 12-inch pizza pan or large cookie sheet.

2. In large bowl, combine pizza crust mix and hot water; stir vigorously with fork about 30 strokes or until blended. Shape dough into ball; coat with 1 teaspoon oil. Cover; let rise in warm place (80 to 85°F.) for 5 minutes.

3. With greased hands, press dough evenly into 9- to 12-inch round on greased pizza pan or cookie sheet. Drizzle dough with melted butter; sprinkle with desired toppings.

4. Bake at 500°F. on lowest oven rack until golden brown. For 9-inch pizza, bake about 12 minutes; for 12-inch pizza, bake about 10 minutes. Remove from cookie sheet. Cool 10 minutes before serving. Cut into wedges.

Yield: 8 servings

Blue Cheese Appetizer Biscuits

Ideal for entertaining, these savory delights are delicious at room temperature and can be made hours before guests arrive. Try them split, spread with mayonnaise and filled with thinly sliced fresh cucumber, tomato or sweet Vidalia onion or roasted red pepper.

Prep Time: 25 minutes

> 2 **cups Martha White® Self-Rising Flour**
> ¼ **cup butter or margarine**
> 4 **oz. blue cheese, crumbled**
> ¾ **cup milk**
> 2 **tablespoons butter or margarine, melted**

1. Heat oven to 450°F. Grease large cookie sheet. Place flour in large bowl. With pastry blender or fork, cut in ¼ cup butter until mixture resembles coarse crumbs. Gently stir in blue cheese. Add milk; stir with fork until soft, moist dough forms and mixture begins to pull away from sides of bowl.

2. On lightly floured surface, knead dough gently just until smooth. Roll out dough to ¼-inch thickness. With sharp knife or pizza cutter, cut into 1½-inch squares. Place biscuits on greased cookie sheet.

3. Bake at 450°F. for 10 to 12 minutes or until light golden brown. Brush hot biscuits with melted butter.

Yield: 36 biscuits

Peppery Benne Seed Wafers and Straws

A cross between biscuits and pie crust, these crisp wafers are flaky and tender. The sesame seed, called benne seed in South Carolina, gives the crackers a nutty flavor.

Prep Time: 30 minutes

> 2 **cups Martha White® Self-Rising Flour**
> ⅓ **cup benne (sesame) seed, toasted***
> ⅛ **teaspoon ground red pepper (cayenne)**
> ¼ **teaspoon pepper**
> ½ **cup cold butter or margarine**
> ½ **cup milk**

1. Heat oven to 425°F. Grease large cookie sheet. In medium bowl, combine flour, benne seed, ground red pepper and pepper; mix well. With pastry blender or fork, cut in butter until mixture resembles coarse crumbs. Add milk; toss and stir lightly with fork. (Mixture will be crumbly.)

2. On lightly floured surface, knead dough just until smooth. Roll out dough to 16x8-inch rectangle, about ¼ inch thick. Cut half of dough into 4x1-inch strips; cut remaining dough into 1½-inch rounds or squares. Place on greased cookie sheet.

3. Bake at 425°F. for 12 to 15 minutes or until light golden brown. Place straws and wafers on wire rack to cool.

Yield: 30 wafers; 16 straws

TIP: * To toast benne seed, spread in shallow baking pan. Bake at 350°F. for 6 to 8 minutes or until golden brown, stirring occasionally. Or place seed in small skillet; cook and stir over medium heat for 8 to 10 minutes or until light golden brown.

Blue Cheese Appetizer Biscuits

Goodness Gracious, It's Good!

"Goodness Gracious, It's Good" appeared on Martha White products and in radio and television advertising for almost 50 years. The embellished "Goodness Gracious, It's Pea-Picking Good" became synonymous with Tennessee Ernie Ford. Today, every Saturday night, the Martha White Grand Ole Opry commercials still end with the catchy slogan: *"Goodness Gracious, It's Good!"*

Cheddar Salsa Biscuit Bites

These tidbits are made like traditional biscuits, except spicy salsa replaces the milk; shredded Cheddar cheese provides great flavor and a crisp texture.

Prep Time: 30 minutes

1⅔ cups Martha White® Self-Rising Flour
4 oz. (1 cup) shredded Cheddar cheese
½ cup salsa
¼ cup butter or margarine, melted
¼ cup water

1. Heat oven to 425°F. Generously grease large cookie sheet. In large bowl, combine flour and cheese; mix well. Add salsa, butter and water; stir just until blended.

2. On lightly floured surface, knead dough gently just until smooth. Press or roll out dough to 12x6-inch rectangle. With sharp knife or pizza cutter, cut into 2x1-inch strips. With thin spatula, place strips about ½ inch apart on greased cookie sheet.

3. Bake at 425°F. for 11 to 13 minutes or until light golden brown. Serve warm.

Yield: 36 biscuit bites

Cheddar Salsa Biscuit Bites

Border Corn Cakes with Black-Eyed Pea Salsa

A great alternative to corn chips, these mini corn cakes are made with a cornbread mix and lots of Cheddar cheese.

Prep Time: 45 minutes

SALSA

1	tablespoon vegetable or olive oil
½	cup chopped onion
2	garlic cloves, minced
2	(15-oz.) cans black-eyed peas, drained
1	cup salsa
1	cup chopped bell pepper
2	medium tomatoes, seeded, chopped
3	tablespoons chopped fresh cilantro
2	tablespoons lemon juice
	Salt and pepper

CORN CAKES

2	(6-oz.) pkg. Martha White® Cotton Pickin' or Buttermilk Cornbread Mix
8	oz. (2 cups) shredded sharp Cheddar cheese
1½	cups milk
1	egg, beaten

1. Heat oil in medium skillet over medium heat until hot. Add onion and garlic; cook until tender, stirring occasionally. Stir in 1 can of the black-eyed peas; cook until thoroughly heated. With potato masher or fork, mash mixture until thick and chunky. Stir in remaining can of peas and the salsa.

2. Remove from heat; stir in all remaining salsa ingredients. Add salt and pepper to taste. Spoon into serving dish. If desired, garnish with additional cilantro. Set aside.

3. Heat griddle or large skillet to medium heat (350°F.). Grease lightly with oil. Griddle is ready when small drops of water sizzle and disappear almost immediately. Pancakes will stick if griddle is too cool. In medium bowl, combine all corn cake ingredients; stir until smooth.

4. For each corn cake, pour heaping tablespoonful batter onto hot griddle. Cook until golden brown on both sides, turning once. If batter thickens, add additional milk. Serve with salsa. Store salsa in refrigerator.

Yield: 36 corn cakes; 5 cups salsa

Old-Fashioned Corn Dogs

Corn dogs may seem a modern marvel, but they're actually an old-fashioned treat you can make at home.

Prep Time: 25 minutes

	Oil or shortening for deep frying
1	cup Martha White® Self-Rising Flour
⅔	cup Martha White® Self-Rising Corn Meal Mix
¾	cup milk
2	tablespoons oil
1	egg, beaten
	Wooden skewers, if desired
1	(1-lb.) pkg. hot dogs
	Mustard and ketchup, if desired

1. In large saucepan or deep fat fryer, heat 2 to 3 inches oil over medium-high heat to 375°F. In medium bowl, combine flour and corn meal mix; mix well. Add milk, 2 tablespoons oil and egg; stir until smooth. Let batter stand at room temperature for 10 minutes.

2. Insert skewers into hot dogs. Dip each hot dog into batter. Carefully lower corn dogs, a few at a time, into hot oil. Cook until golden brown and corn dogs float to surface. Drain on paper towels. Serve hot with mustard and ketchup.

Yield: 10 corn dogs

Border Corn Cakes with Black-Eyed Pea Salsa